TAKE THIS

LIFE

AND

LOVE IT!

TAKE THIS
LIFE
AND
LOVE IT!

(53) Ways to Help You Do Just That

TOM LAWHEAD

Published by Advantage, Charleston, South Carolina.
Member of Advantage Media Group.

ADVANTAGE is a registered trademark and the Advantage colophon is a trademark of Advantage Media Group, Inc.

Printed in the United States of America.

ISBN: 978-1-59932-466-1
LCCN: 2013955464

This publication is designed to provide accurate and authoritative information in regard to the subject matter covered. It is sold with the understanding that the publisher is not engaged in rendering legal, accounting, or other professional services. If legal advice or other expert assistance is required, the services of a competent professional person should be sought.

 Advantage Media Group is proud to be a part of the Tree Neutral® program. Tree Neutral offsets the number of trees consumed in the production and printing of this book by taking proactive steps such as planting trees in direct proportion to the number of trees used to print books. To learn more about Tree Neutral, please visit www.treeneutral.com. To learn more about Advantage's commitment to being a responsible steward of the environment, please visit www.advantagefamily.com/green

Advantage Media Group is a publisher of business, self-improvement, and professional development books and online learning. We help entrepreneurs, business leaders, and professionals share their Stories, Passion, and Knowledge to help others Learn & Grow. Do you have a manuscript or book idea that you would like us to consider for publishing? Please visit advantagefamily.com or call 1.866.775.1696.

Dedication

To my brothers Allen, Mike and Doug
and sympathies to wives Ronda, Becky and Diane

....

Unity Through Humility

If there be therefore any consolation in Christ, if any comfort of love, if any fellowship of the Spirit, if any bowels and mercies, Fulfil ye my joy, that ye be likeminded, having the same love, being of one accord, of one mind. Let nothing be done through strife or vainglory; but in lowliness of mind let each esteem other better than themselves. Look not every man on his own things, but every man also on the things of others. Let this mind be in you, which was also in Christ Jesus.

—Philippians 2:1-5

Contents

Preface

THIS BOOK TURNED OUT TO BE far more serious than I ever intended. Originally, my energy was focused on producing a somewhat humorous book about living life to its fullest—in other words, a party-time book.

Somewhere along the way, I felt moved by a higher author to change gears. My focus shifted completely. I was driven to open up my entire life, good and bad, to strangers everywhere and provide some real-life solutions and happiness in their lives. This book is now an attempt to give a diverse audience a sense of what a very average family faces every day and how to deal with it.

We are all going to make some serious mistakes in our lives. I think this is the way God planned it. That being said, I've come to the conclusion, he is not concentrating on our mistakes, but he wants to see if we are willing to ask for his help. It's that simple. That's the way I see it.

What I've Figured Out

Where do I begin? Writing this book has completely drained me in every way possible. I told my brothers, since I'm already a professional musician and not an author, it would have been a whole lot easier to write an album of songs than do this. Probably be more popular and profitable too.

For all of those would-be authors, and I know there is one on every street corner, pay close attention to the following:

This is a journey and not a project. Putting my life on paper has been one of the most difficult and challenging experiences imaginable, but unbelievably rewarding and satisfying!

I am really overwhelmed by the responses I get when I tell someone, especially total strangers, that I am writing a book. Their first response is to ask, "What's it about?" Then I either hear, "I'm thinking about writing one," or "I need to write a book." What is it about writing a book? My book started out as a total joke because I hated people who wrote books! You'll see why shortly.

Again, if you are even remotely thinking about writing a book, think again. Unless you are like all those famous people who have somebody write their book for them, or you are a professional author, this isn't as fun and glamorous as you might think.

Enough about all my pain.

I do have to admit I can't wait to go around town telling everybody,

"I wrote a book!"

Biggest Lessons Here?

I've figured out you can take this life and love it!

What does that really mean? When I started to write this book, I would keep a notepad nearby to jot down thoughts that would just come to me anytime or anywhere. I made a list of some of the more interesting topics and thought I would share them at the end of this journey to see if I have shed any light on what I was trying to accomplish—kind of a self-exam.

So here it goes. Let's see how I did. Most of these thoughts were written on stained napkins or business cards and barely legible.

DIE BROKE AND ENJOY IT!

Actually, I had planned my life out to avoid spending everything before I died. The year 2008 has made this more of a challenge, but I think I'm going to pull it off, assuming I don't live past my budget or we have another 2008. I don't plan on leaving a whole lot of money lying around. My motto, "Leave no dollar behind." Sorry, relatives.

I SHOULD HAVE …

Volunteered more, mentored more, tithed more, gone to church more, pursued more of a professional music career with my brothers—I know we had the talent; we just got sidetracked by life. Plus, my dad always discouraged us from pursuing music as a full-time profession—tried to change the world, been a better influence on my nephews and nieces, taken better care of my body,

…paid somebody to write this book for me!

I SHOULDN'T HAVE…

Started drinking at age 14, abused alcohol, tried drugs, driven a car after drinking alcohol, given up on politics, invested so much in one stock, stolen anything, cheated in school, trusted the wrong people, lied about so many things.

CALCULATING THE COST OF WORRY?

I can't find the formula. Let's just say it's *really* expensive and there are no refunds or exchanges. Don't worry about how much it's costing you; just stop it. Worrying has never solved anything.

By the way, how in the hell do you convince somebody to stop worrying?

Find some way to get your mind on another subject, when you start to worry. Consciously distract yourself with thoughts far removed from your problem. Immediately try to think of something good that just happened or is about to. You can try alcohol and drugs — but man, trust me, they are temporary and expensive.

The greatest solution to worry on this earth is prayer.

THE PAST AND THE FUTURE

One is over. One just started. Learn from the past but stay out of it. Concentrate on today. You have all day tomorrow to think about the future.

I personally have a real problem forgetting about the past. I mean it can haunt the heck out of me. It's like Satan keeps coming up to me and saying, "Hey, Tom, remember the other day when ..." On and on and the more I try to get it out of my head, the more he keeps talking and talking. Satan never wants to remind me of all the wonderful things that have happened in the past. If you analyze this in biblical terms, we really don't have a past if we seek God's forgiveness.

If you get too bogged down in the future, your old buddy, worry, will pop his head right out. My whole book, to some degree, concerns itself with the future and to some degree with the past, but I like to think that what I am encouraging and promoting is preparation and planning. Bottom line: Not much you can do about the past. Live today and look forward to the future.

LOVE AND ROMANCE

Love is one of the most wonderful gifts you can give and receive! Usually and hopefully, the more you give, the more you receive. Try both. I highly recommend it.

Romance is not to be wasted. Use it every day. You will be glad you did. Be natural when you attempt this. Be aware of what your partner's idea of romance is. Ask. Find out what excites your partner or doesn't. Men need to double or triple what they consider to be romancing.

If romance has disappeared in the relationship, it is a major problem. Let's hope it was there in the beginning, for a reason. Don't avoid addressing this. I just can't imagine what it would be like to not have both of these flourishing in the relationship. Man, that's *gotta* be awkward. Probably not too much fun either.

INSPIRATION/PERSPIRATION

Provided by true leaders and comes from following them. There is nothing like hearing someone giving an inspirational speech or a preacher giving an inspirational sermon. How do they do it? They have to be committed to a cause. I think it would be very hard to fake inspiration, even though some do.

I love being around people who are inspired. It's contagious. Perspiration is what you produce when you act on inspiration.

MONEY AND FINANCE

Earn it, save it and spend it wisely. Hey, I wrote a whole chapter on this. Read ahead.

Please don't let money be the center of your universe. Think of all the horrible things you see on the news and read in the paper. Every one of them can somehow be related back to money. That should tell you something.

I'll be the first to admit, everything takes money, but who said you had to have everything? Seriously, don't become obsessed with it. Do not worry about the Joneses. Money destroys marriage more than anything else. The last thing I'll say about money is *don't waste it.*

FAILURE

It happens. Get over it. Don't make it a habit. It's contagious. I'm not going to bore you or remind you of all the famous, brilliant and successful people who literally thrived on failure, but they're out there.

I think some people confuse failure with quitters. I can't stand quitters! Now talk about losers, give me a quitter and I'll give you a loser and a failure, every time. Failure is a learning curve. It is to be respected, learned from and acted on. Nothing like a good failure to get the juices going. Now I'm not encouraging failure, but it sure does make me stronger.

FAMILY

It's everything. Keep reading. If you're not speaking to a family member, for whatever reason, or have just stopped communicating, be the one to reopen that door. I can't add up all the times my brothers and I would get into some pretty mean knock-down drag-outs, but at some point, one of us would take that bold step. It doesn't matter whose fault something was or why something happened. Forgiveness is a blessing, not a curse. More about this at the end of my book.

FRIENDS

Can't live without them. Respect and cherish them. Give more than you get.

I have to add, do not let them take advantage of you or make you do something you know is not right. There are times when their influence can be questionable. Of course, then they should no longer be your friends.

The best friends I ever had are my three brothers and they still are. I like to think that our other friends learned something from us about friendship and family. Maybe somewhere along the way they got jealous or envious of us and became closer to their siblings. Who knows? I hope so.

RELIGION

Give your life to Jesus Christ. Respect others' beliefs. Avoid hypocrisy.

Share the spirit.

I never was much of a churchgoer, if that's a word. Maybe it was my childhood memories of church. Remember, I hated regular school, so I guess I just naturally had a dislike for Sunday school and church.

I have realized how important it is in my adult life. Many of my friends consider themselves good Christians but don't feel the impor-tance of physically attending church. I have to admit it is one of the tougher things for me to commit to on a regular basis, but I keep improving. We, as Christians, need to gather together to share God's word. You can't do that in your living room.

POLITICS

Avoid it. If you have the time and the stomach, go for it. Just know what you're getting yourself into. I know I'm a coward. I should try to change things. Maybe I'll add "politics" to one of my "should haves …." I used to be a "news junkie." I could not get enough of it. I would have three different TVs going with news shows just so I wouldn't miss anything. Somehow I thought this was making me smarter. Duh! Just the opposite. Problem is I would get almost physically sick listening to politicians all day. This was also a bad habit of my dad's. I think that is where I got it. Thankfully, I have broken away from all that crap and listen to music instead.

LEADERSHIP: WHERE HAVE ALL THE LEADERS GONE?

Read *Atlas Shrugged*. Who is John Galt? Contribute if you can. Give back. Try to be the best leader you can. If you own your own business or manage others and you find a leader, don't let him get away. Leadership without responsibility is dangerous. It demands accountability too.

Exceptional leaders are rare these days. My concern is the type of leader out there now. Personal agendas and special interest and greed have overtaken leaders of today. How do we get back on track? Somewhere along the way leaders have forgotten who the ultimate leader is: God!

THE FAIRNESS OF LIFE

Don't try to measure it. Don't try to compare how much fairness you get versus your neighbor. Ever heard the phrase, "Damn! That ain't fair"? Get over it. If you feel you have been cheated or treated unfairly, chances are you did something to cause it. People who constantly worry about fairness usually end up being my next topic: losers.

LOSERS, WHAT WOULD WE DO WITHOUT THEM?

Try to be a good mentor to those who seem to lose more than others. Be a gracious winner. Some of my best friends are losers. I just said that because it sounds funny.

By the way, how do you define loser? I really don't know. I know one thing: I don't want to be one. Seriously, I don't like the word and I recommend you try not to use it.

DEATH

Unavoidable. If you're like me, and you have lived every day like you've loved it and given your life to Christ, you won't fear death. It's actually that simple.

Hopefully, you continually and daily think about the spiritual side of death. What would happen to you if you did die today? Do you know where you would end up? Is this it? Pretty serious stuff.

If I were you, I would make sure I had a good feeling about this. Not much more I can add.

Introduction

I AM A BIG FAN of the famous comedian and late-night talk-show host Stephen Colbert, and I too "am no fan of books," as he so elegantly stated in the beginning of his first and only book, *I Am America (and So Can You)*.

In 2008 I printed 100 copies of a book called *Live While You're Still Alive!!!* The unique part of that book was that all 200 pages were intentionally left blank. It was a joke — and an expensive one — but a blast and a great success. Everyone loved the cover, the inserts and the reviews. I made them all up. Most of my friends use copies as coffee table books or keep them in their office for a quick laugh with associates or clients. Let's face it. It's a conversation piece and who reads all these books people buy, anyway? Mission accomplished. Oh, and I did send a copy to my dear friend Mr. Colbert, which was immediately returned, unopened.

This joke was my personal attack on everyone writing a book about anything and especially nothing. Aren't you just sick of hearing about everybody's "new book?" And they're all best sellers! Some of these books are completed and on shelves before the authors even say they are going to write a book. In some cases I actually think they didn't know they'd written a book. How does that happen? The final straw for me was the best seller of actor, singer, and so on, Miley Cyrus, on her life's experiences by age 14. Oh, and Mr. O'Reilly, no more books, please! Please!

I retired at age 39 and after 16 years of retirement, at age 55, I have basically done everything I could possibly want to do, and I did some things more than once. Now you may say that can't be true. Maybe it's a little exaggeration. I probably have missed a lot of things, but you miss my point. I'm out there trying hard to get it all in. What's the old saying about regrets on your death bed? Well, I really don't remember it. As a matter of fact, I don't think I ever heard it.

After college, I started on the management training program at what was the state's largest bank at the time, and while employed, held about every job you could have at a bank. During this same time, I was a professional musician, performing all over South Carolina, North Carolina and Georgia. I started performing for money at age 14. That's over 40 years ago! No wonder everything on me hurts.

Now let's get back to why I should write a book after all my "book-writer bashing."

It's simple. It's a monumental challenge to write a successful book (best seller) by a complete unknown stranger from basically nowhere! He really didn't accomplish much other than spiritual fulfillment with God, overwhelming family blessings and a lifetime of friends. He also managed to have an average business and was moderately financially successful with some pretty funny, sad and valuable experiences. And he just somehow ended up happy and fulfilled in all this mess in a relatively short period of time, with plenty of life left. Sounds dull and boring? Can't learn from this? Not *gonna* sell? Let's fool everybody. Buy it!

Just imagine it. He's not famous. He's not a hero. And he ain't a crook. He's not a murderer. He's no athlete. He's not a politician. He's not an actor. No talk show host. He's no chef. He's not a rock star (wanted to be). He's not a preacher. He's not a motivational speaker. And finally, he's not an overnight successful kazillionaire entrepreneur. Again, not a chance. Ain't *gonna* sell.

Looked like an overwhelming task, so I went to a marketer/publisher with my idea.

The most awakening advice that I walked away with was from the CEO. "The worst way to make money selling a book is to sell it in a book store." Now what in the hell am I *gonna* do? According to most statistics, the average Joe who writes a book, will sell an average of 2000 books over his lifetime with an average profit of $2 per book. You can do the math. That's not counting the cost of publishing it. Money loser.

So, he is right. If you are just an "average Joe," it won't work. You have to be one of those guys I mentioned earlier to have a best seller. Who said life is fair? The CEO did share with me some excellent ways to make money writing books, but that's for another day.

Well, let's just say I'd like to prove the experts wrong. Bear with me while I attempt to tell you who I am, why I'm writing this book and what the reader can take from it. Fair enough?

This new author is a 55-year-old man, happily married to his high-school homecoming queen in "little ole" Irmo, South Carolina. We live on a large lake in Lexington, South Carolina, with our 20-year-old kitten, Daisy.

My career was primarily in the financial services industry. I held positions as a corporate and business banker as well as a private financial advisor. I also spent several years in the investment banking business. I was an entrepreneur at heart but way too afraid to take the financial, physical, mental, and so on, risk. So I lived vicariously through all my clients.

What do I do all day long now? I play guitar and sing in nursing homes, adult day-care facilities and special needs hospitals, three days a week, with my brother Doug and a friend, Pastor Dave Simpson.

The Faith Brothers

We affectionately call ourselves the Faith Brothers. I've come full circle, from playing in night clubs all night long for lots of money to performing all morning in health care facilities for free! Now that's life changing, an experience I will share in more detail at the end of my book.

My brothers and I have recently put some of our old band back together and have named it the Lawhead Brothers' Reunion Band. The other two members include Carlos Gibbons (whom my mother affectionately considered her fifth Lawhead boy) on trumpet. On drums is Mike's brother-in-law "Boogie" Weatherford. We are back playing for private functions and country clubs, and so on. Needless to say, I have plenty to occupy my time.

The Lawhead Brothers tape cover

My beautiful wife, Diane, is a registered nurse at the local hospital. We have no children — but loads of siblings, nephews and nieces. Both my overwhelmingly influential parents are deceased, with Diane's mother still actively living out life. My three older brothers are my closest and dearest friends. My oldest brother, Allen, is a gynecological oncologist in Atlanta, Georgia, and one of the best singer/guitar players around. Mike is the director/physician of an urgent care hospital in Blythewood, South Carolina, and a killer sax player, while Doug is a full-time volunteer for various churches, nursing and adult care organizations, and special needs hospitals in Columbia, South Carolina. And he is the greatest bass player to be found. I forgot to mention myself: I am retired, a volunteer and an average singer and guitar player. So there you have it: who I am, the youngest of the four infamous Lawhead brothers.

This story is being told to share the lifetime of an average family that managed to accomplish above-average success and failures and to guide families, young and old, through what God has told us would be a challenging journey. Can you really believe it? An average family with some invaluable insight, perspective and lessons to help you navigate God's plan. "Say it ain't so." Read on.

My most important challenge in writing this book is insuring that you personally take something of value away from it. I can candidly tell you that just spending the time I have spent preparing these pages has changed me forever. Going back through all the memories of so many experiences and trying to tie everything together in a single book has been an indescribable journey and just plain hard to do. This book was not written overnight, nor should it be read overnight. It is truly a lifetime that has been reconstructed to help others. Try reading a chapter and sleep on it as you reflect and compare it to your own personal experiences.

My life has benefited substantially by just writing this book. So how can it not have some impact on a total stranger? I hope you can walk through this and literally feel the emotions of the stories, and more important, use them as lessons in your own life. Then, it's "Mission accomplished!" again.

I will take this a step further and encourage parents to begin putting together stories like the ones they will read in this book for their own families. I have a dear friend who has just done this for his family. He has put together little lessons about how to just be happy. What a great way to share your experience with your families while you're still alive. Do it while you can and your memory is still somewhat fresh.

Let's get serious for a moment. I don't want to spoil the story, but these are just a few of some of the **"takeaways"** of this book:

- The first one is the importance of God in you and your family's life (no exception!). It is never too late to accept Jesus Christ as your lord and savior. Prayer works.

- Stop and think about the proportion of time you spend making a particular decision, compared to the importance of that decision. (Read this again!).

- Make discipline a priority in your household from the very beginning.

- It is never too late to make adjustments in your life. And I mean big adjustments if necessary.

- Get over mistakes, disappointments and failures. Your mind will never let you completely stop looking back, so just glance occasionally and move on.

- My favorite: Stop worrying and at least do something about it or shut up.

- Importance of planning.

- Value of caring about others.

- Start saving money before you can walk.

- The value of pretax investing and compounding.

- Life is not always understandable or fair. Handicaps and tragedies can be overcome.

- **Awaken people.** Don't live for retirement; live now.

- I think some people should have **three dates on their tombstone:**

  - **First date:** When you were born.

  - **Second date:** When you stopped living—but you didn't die; you just lost all desires and started existing—no drive, emotion or purpose. I see this a lot where I perform. I think there is a cure for this and it starts with family.

- **Third date:** Actual death.

- I talk about this in my afterword, but it's too important not to mention now: *reconcile family differences before it's too late*, the earlier the better. You take the lead. **Be the "silent hero."**

- As a wrap up, *forgiveness is a must*. Make the best of your imperfections. Competition can be healthy and losing is not dying. Try to have fun with yourself and others and never lose sight of humor. It's contagious and healthy. Almost forgot: don't let technology render you socially dysfunctional.

- Finally, my attempt in this book is to give you a semiautobiographical sketch of my life. How I managed to incorporate the things and events that happened to me, good and bad, into living a full and satisfied life, with few regrets and tons of friends, family and happiness.

My journey is far from over and I plan to continue to "take this life and love it."

Chapter One

Growing Kids Not Shrubs

My family originated in Richmond, Virginia. We moved to Lynchburg, after my three older brothers were born and I was on the way in 1958. My mother and father were in their late thirties when I was born and they could not have been more opposite.

My dad was tall and lean and very soft-spoken, while my mother was short, stout and very bubbly. They were the perfect couple! When it came to raising their four boys, who were all born within six years of each other, these were the basic rules of life:

Mom: "Losing is not an option."

Dad: "Son, do your best."

Well, that pretty much tells it all. It was that way for the rest of our lives and I mean forever. This went on until their death. Dad passed at 81 in 2003 and my mother, at 86, in 2012.

I guess in their defense I need to briefly describe the parents who raised, molded and shaped the infamous Lawhead brothers.

My mother was a stay-at-home mom until we all started grade school and she pretty much wore the pants in the family. That was, until there was something big or controversial that needed my dad's hand. He could lay down the law when needed. Speaking of hands, he was not too bad with the old hand on the backside either. Don't want to get too sidetracked, but this does bring up the all-important issue of early discipline. I'll share my experiences with discipline shortly.

Now, let's get back to my story about those parents of mine.

My mother never met a stranger and truly loved everybody and it showed. There was nothing artificial about her. She was the real deal. She had absolutely no musical or artistic talent, but boy, what an entertainer. She could work a crowd like you've never seen. By the time she left somewhere, she knew your name, your mother's name, children, where you went to church, social security number and on and on!

I give my mother most of the credit for my social and promotional skills as well as my self-confidence and fierce competitiveness. She was a salesman and negotiator too.

Eventually, later in her life, **she had to have both her legs amputated** due to diabetes, but I swear, **I think it speeded her up.**

My father, on the other hand, was an incredible musician, gifted artist and mental genius. He was the kindest man I ever knew. My mother used to joke, "If someone ever ran over your father with a car, he would get up and apologize for getting in the way." That was my dad. Oh, what a great influence on us boys.

I could always count on him for everything and I never wanted to disappoint him or let him down. I can proudly say I never remember my dad putting pressure on me to accomplish anything or be a huge success at something. All he would do is give encouragement, advice, compliments and counsel when needed. It wasn't what you did or accomplished but how you did it.

I give my father credit for my character, integrity and humility.

I mean, we boys had some good genes. How could we go wrong? All we needed to do was somehow mix the two attributes of both parents into one, and we would have the world on a string.

Joking aside, **it was a true blessing that our parents were so completely different and diverse,** and more importantly, showed us the importance of love in a relationship that lasted a lifetime. That love was also uncompromising and undying when it came to their four boys. Love surrounded our home, in between all the knock-down drag-out fights.

Let me share some personal experiences that I had with my family. They have lasted a lifetime for me and I would like to pass them down to younger moms and dads and to grandparents for reflection. I have broken them into separate categories for simplicity.

Competition. Now the dark side of all this touchy, lovey stuff.

Let the games begin. If there were one word I had to choose to describe my relationship with my three older brothers, it would be competition. I give my mother credit for this, while my dad actually discouraged it. The fact that we were all so close in age also intensified things and made them pretty exciting.

Everything we did was a competition. Chess, monopoly, checkers, all sports, music, taking out the trash, breathing, and so on, and "the all-important school grades!" Yes, the presentation of the report card was quite an event at our house. Notice I refer to house, not home, during this exercise. This was fierce competition. No place for niceties. The environment was hostile, not homely. We were more concerned about sharing our grades with each other than with our parents. That just doesn't make any sense, but that's the way it was. My parents never had to discuss grades with us, ever. We boys managed to keep everything in perfect balance, with our own self-policing and competition.

Parents need to realize this was healthy and controlled to some degree but very effective. Let's just say all four of us were pretty much A students. Nobody wanted to bring home anything less.

When we played games, they could last for days. No one, and I mean no one, wanted to lose. If you were losing, you would do almost anything just to keep the game alive. Cheating I'm sure existed but was rarely penalized.

None of us were good losers. In fact, it was literally hell to lose. The winner would relish his victory for days. The loser would usually retaliate with physical attacks or verbal attacks and explanations of how the winner must have cheated to win.

Competition is an extremely healthy thing when kept in check. Again, my parents were almost always there to make sure things didn't get out of hand.

My competitive nature, learned at such an early age, made it very easy for me to be successful as an adult.

Discipline. I still, until this day, don't know how my parents always found out about things we boys did that needed remediation. We always blamed it on my brother Doug, who was affectionately known as **Jimmy the Weasel.** From what I understand, I think there is one in every family.

Regardless of how they knew or found out, justice was always carried out. Now we all had pretty different opinions of the term *justice*. Needless to say, no bad deed was left unpunished. And there was nothing more entertaining than to be able to sit and watch one of the brothers accept his punishment. It was truly a spectator sport in our family. I believe to this day that it was completely intentional on my parents' part to make this a family event.

I give both my parents tremendous credit for instilling in all four of us an absolute respect for discipline and to understand the consequences of a lack of it.

Discipline, I'm sad to say, has gotten lost in our families today, as well as our schools and society in general. Not *gonna* get on a soapbox, but this is where the family has the potential to either prosper or fail.

Let me kind of repeat myself: **Discipline will either make or break a family**. Bottom line: Please, stop reading right now and think about what I just said. Think about your own family situation. It is not about how much or how little discipline. It is about how it is managed and administered, or if it exists at all. Stop!

I wish I had the recipe that worked for all families, but it's just not that simple.

But I do know what worked for my folks raising four rowdy boys. It wasn't perfect by any stretch, but they did everything they could to be:

Consistent, fair, equitable, reasonable and immediate. That ain't easy, but you *gotta* try it and get better at it every day. No excuses. If you have problems with this, you go get some help, fast! I know there are all kinds of different circumstance today, but that's no excuse for letting this get out of control.

If you can't handle your child or children, get help somewhere, before it destroys the whole family. If one particular child needs extra attention or is substantially affecting the entire family and you can't control the situation, seek professional help.

If you don't get a handle on this early, the rest of this book is a waste.

Whoa! Glad to get that off my chest and over with.

Sunday school/church. One word: *mandatory*. No discussion, comments or excuses. Oh, I almost forgot three more words: life or death. Not a whole lot more to say about this subject. My mom and dad both taught Sunday school. **God was the center of our life and he was there to stay.**

You were not physically punished for not going to church, but it was a mental torment. That was worse. Oh, and no activities that day, either.

Christmas. At our home Christmas, commonly pronounced "chaos," was an indescribable evening and early morning of emotional highs and lows like no other human has known, the anticipation and excitement brewing at unsustainable levels. Yet there was a calmness and peace upstairs where my parents would be, somehow peacefully asleep.

The lesson here is that all four boys never questioned Santa's existence or motives and welcomed him with an abundance of love but were never able to catch him

The Lawhead brothers on Christmas

coming down the chimney though they tried every year. Now, how do parents pull that off? Well, they did and I loved them for that. You never saw four boys as happy for each other as each one was for himself. Now that is true love. These are experiences you carry with you your entire life. How can any parent not understand the importance of the togetherness this one day provides? **Unconditional love between siblings is a true blessing.**

Store night. Now this was an event you never—and I mean never—missed. Every Friday evening my dad would load the four of us up in the station wagon and head for the Tommy Freeze convenience store. Boy, the memories there. It was locally owned and my dad knew all the folks up there. It was a little gathering hole.

Now I've seen magicians in my life and a few so-called miracle workers, but my dad worked incredible magic with his one dollar. We had hours to shop and decide what each of us would spend our 25 cents on. How did he convince us that 25 cents was a lot of money? Talk about decision making. Sometimes we would pool our money to buy something a little more expensive and share. Talk about close brothers. Meanwhile, dad was busy having a cold one with the owner and talking about how tough life was. Somehow, by the end of the night, both of them managed to forget about the worries of the world, while we were just happy to be there and clueless to what was going on outside the store.

Fishing on the river. Either Saturday or Sunday or both, the gang was going fishing, no matter what. These are incredible memories that will never leave you. My poor dad would get up, after we dragged him out of bed, to get all the fishing gear together, and off we would go. Well, it wasn't quite that simple. We could never find all the cane poles or have the tackle we needed, and so on. Our first stop was the "nasty ole bait shop" to get our fresh worms and crickets. Oh, and dad would buy one old Black Label beer to last the whole afternoon. He kept it in a little brown paper bag.

It never failed that one of us would slip and fall in the river every time we went fishing. It was almost like we took turns. Dad would have to go in after us. It was actually pretty funny and fortunately, **no casualties.**

One weekend we would fish on the Broad River and the next, we would fish on the Saluda River. Both were nearby and only a few miles apart. Each was uniquely different and spectacular.

I'll never forget one day overhearing one of our neighbors talking to my dad about our yard while we were waiting in the wagon to

go fishing. He was trying to politely ask him about keeping his lawn and shrubs a little neater. My dad looked back at his car full of boys and cane poles and grinned and politely told the neighbor that he was a little **too busy raising boys, not shrubs,** and thanked him for his concern.

Boys ready for fishing

That was the last we ever heard about the yard. I've always hoped that day might have had some influence on our neighbor because it sure did on us boys!

Annual beach vacation. Myrtle Beach, South Carolina, it was. No exception here, either. Every August, off we would go on an adventure ride no one can really describe or explain without being there. Picture a very old, half-broken-down, Chevrolet station wagon with no air conditioning, or any extras, for that matter. What should be a three-hour trip usually lasted at least five. There were stops and there were stops and more stops. Stops were made for every reason possible. The boys fighting was a favorite. Food, drinks and bathroom. There were all kinds of animals we needed to get out to see.

We would go out to dinner every night we were there and that provided entertainment and chaos everywhere we went. **Nothing was easy or simple.**

One of the main reasons we went to the beach was to compete in a very big annual swimming meet for all the top swimmers in the state. In was a mad house with thousands of swimmers everywhere, but what a blast!

Haircuts from hell. This borders on child abuse. But I'll share it anyway. Being a typical middle-class family, we were always trying to cut corners. Having four boys didn't help matters. Well, about once a month, my dad would attempt to cut our hair on a Saturday afternoon. First, he thought he knew how to cut hair and second, he didn't. To make matters worse, he would start taking a little nip of whiskey before he started. The trick for us was to try to get to the front of the line on haircut day. Let's just say that you could easily tell at the end of the day where you had been in line. You see, my dad would keep taking those little nips of whiskey while he was cutting hair. We still laugh to this day about my brother Mike's haircut the day before the school yearbook pictures were to be taken. Dad had done a real botched job on Mike and **he looked like a sheered opossum.** You've never heard such crying and that was my just my mother. We still have the yearbook picture and bring it out every Christmas for a lot of laughs. It never gets old—unless you're Mike.

Mike's haircut from hell!

Music lessons. My dad was a hell of a musician. He played everything and had a voice that was truly mesmerizing. He started teaching us to play all kinds of instruments almost before we could walk. He would sing us all to bed at night with his guitar and that smooth voice. We all later joined the school band and continued our music careers.

My dad had a piece of equipment that was literally magic when it came to teaching us music or almost anything, for that matter. It was a very old reel-to-reel tape player and recorder with a microphone. He would tape us singing, playing sax, guitar, ukulele or just plain talking and we couldn't wait to hear ourselves. I think my dad actually had more fun with the microphone than we did. He would have a little of his home-made beer he brewed in our basement and start chatting with us on the microphone like he was interviewing us. I still have some of those old recordings, which are priceless—me singing, at the top of my lungs, at four years old. What a hoot!

Kindergarten. I'll cut to the chase. I was madly in love with my kindergarten teacher. I can't even remember her name now, but back then she was everything and she was beautiful.

Kindergarten class

My teacher knew that I could sing and asked me to sing for the class one day. I acted shy, but I couldn't believe this was happening. She also offered me a silver dollar to sing the song "Old Shep." It was one of her favorite songs and one my dad had taught me when I was four, so I had it down pretty pat. My performance was a hit and after that I would sing to the class several times a month, with a different song and a new silver dollar, only now, I requested that I got to scratch her back as I sang. She loved to have her back scratched and we all fought over that chance.

Can you believe it? **Kindergarten, money, women and fame?**

I realized then that music was my ticket and would set the stage for me being an entertainer the rest of my life.

I also share this story as a precursor to my later, entrepreneurial tendencies.

All these events appear to primarily involve my father. Nothing could be further from the truth. My mother orchestrated all of these activities to the very tee. None of this would have been remotely possible without her diligent planning and preparation before all these events took place. They were truly a team that managed to use each other's talents and expertise to enable us to live life to its fullest. They provided constant entertainment with almost no financial means to do so. We were one big happy family!

The end to this chapter was written after I completed it, and it is an awkward end at that, but, something I find overwhelming, discomforting and almost unforgivable not to talk about when discussing families. I've never really paid much attention to it until now. Read on.

I mentioned early on, that I am not an admirer of authors nor an avid book reader, but while writing this book. I did find myself reading and browsing dozens and dozens of books to get an idea of what I liked and didn't like about books in general.

One very disturbing trend I saw in several of these books was stories of tragic childhoods that basically destroyed the writers' young adult life and had profound impact on their entire lives. Some of these people overcame these atrocities, while others just lived to later tell about their experiences and warn others.

I'm speaking primarily of sexual, physical and mental torment, rape and abuse, most of which was inflicted by relatives, family members, babysitters, occasionally strangers, and so on. The victim was too afraid to confide in anyone while the abuse continued. The blame could be placed almost anywhere, but that's not my point.

I guess I'm trying to understand why someone, somewhere did not scream out about these horrible events. Could any of this been avoided or stopped **by having both parents constantly involved with their children?** I don't know.

Then I wonder, could this have somehow happened in my household? I look back and feel strongly that the relationship we had with our parents and between siblings would have enabled us to run to someone for help. At the very least, we would have known that something that was not right was happening and needed to be stopped.

That was obviously not the case for the children in many of the books I read, and that horrifies me. What went wrong? How could it have happened?

My only reason for even including this short excerpt is to make parents aware of the potential for such devastation. How do you know if this is happening in your house? I don't know and can't relate to these poor victims who have suffered these nightmares and will for the rest of their lives. I guess with my rambling I'm saying, for God's sake **be aware of what goes on in your house or another's house** when your children's lives are at stake.

There goes another soap box. Didn't have any fun writing this part, but if it makes one parent or child listen, mission accomplished!

Let's Talk Takeaways

1. God was always part of our family and always will be.

2. From the very beginning there was a very early showing and promoting of love between parent/child and siblings. Love filled our house and you knew it. Don't teach love; show it and live by example.

3. Your children are keenly aware of your relationship with your spouse, trust me. Know and realize that and don't ever lose sight of it.

4. Discipline. It is a make or break deal. Don't provide excuses for a lack of it. You decide. Need help? Don't wait.

5. Competition. Healthy. Don't fear it. Bring it on. Pays off big time later in life.

6. If a parent senses anything unusual or a change in a child's behavior, do not ignore. Be nosey. Don't let abuse go unnoticed or repeated.

7. Know who is with your children at all times. One mistake could cost a lifetime of regrets for everyone and especially your child.

8. Raise children, not lawns.

Chapter Two

The Value of Leadership and the Responsibility and Accountability It Demands

I knew early on I had a knack for sales and negotiating skills. Remember, good ole mom. Somehow, I began to realize that we were not rich. Maybe it was the 25 cents for store night. I figured it was up to me to provide the majority of my spending money.

There were some great memories of getting together with my buddies each week when we would trade toys and things at each other's homes. Well, I would always come out on top and get the best of everybody. My mother would sometime get phone calls from my friends' mothers asking if they could get back some items their sons shouldn't have traded or that might not have been exactly an even trade. What a shyster! Then I would get a lecture on ethics from my parents. But, even with that, I loved the art of the deal.

Let me bore you with some of the favorite entrepreneurial avenues I followed on my way to early wealth:

Selling peanuts at the University of South Carolina college football games. One of my pals got me this gig and fortunately, his mother was supportive and a great taxi driver. My folks tolerated it. Not a bad setup. We busted our butts for three-quarters of the game and sat on our fannies the fourth quarter to watch. It could get old shouting, "Peanuts, peanuts, get your fresh peanuts." Sometimes I would shout, "One bag for half the price of two," just to make it interesting and fun. The intoxicated ones fell for it.

Just think, making good money selling nuts gets you free admission to a college football game, never having to worry about not getting a ticket to the game and then to top it off, eventually, a view of the game from every section of the stadium. I made a pretty good living each fall, but it was tough, sweaty work. Lesson here: if you're *gonna* work hard, find some perks that go with it.

Babysitting was not one of my favorite opportunities, but I guess I could say it was pretty easy money. I never did the "infant thing" and handled mostly kids almost my age and—can you believe it?—some older than me. That didn't make sense, but who's asking? I guess I was being paid to entertain their kids while they were out. Once again there were food and beverage **perks with this job and no overhead.**

Paper drive director was not a paying job and was designed as volunteer work to raise money for the school. Several times a year the elementary school would have those old-fashioned paper drives at which all the moms would drive the largest vehicle the family owned—

back then, the traditional station wagon—filled with months and months of newspapers and magazines. They would unload the car at the front of the school, with my assistance, along with my other staff of volunteers.

Well that was all fine and good and we did raise a lot of money for the school. Somehow along the way, as director, I began to notice certain magazines. They were hidden in these mounds of newspapers that caught my eye as I was sorting piles. I began collecting these—I guess you would say, "girlie magazines"—on my own and storing them in a box for later review. After a while, I realized they had some value for some of my other classmates. So I began selling them. That lasted about a year until the "feds"—Mom and Dad—shut down operations. Another ethics lesson! The point here is that I did do some bad things, **but my parents were there to correct me and try to teach me what I did wrong, why it was wrong and not to do it again. Managed discipline.**

Early politics. The salesman in me naturally flowed over to politics. By the end of my middle-school years—that's eighth grade—I had been president, vice president and treasurer of the school. I was also editor of the newspaper as well as the art director for the paper. I forgot to mention that my dad was also a wonderful artist and taught us all to draw.

What I gained during this part of my life was the value of leadership and the respect that came with it, something that was not to be abused, taken for granted or wasted. Unfortunately, later in life, I became very disillusioned with politics. More detail later.

Yep, that's me!

I feel compelled to add some very personal aspects of my adolescence, which were in some ways distracting and uncomfortable to deal with. You might say I had some issues with my personal appearance. Now, you are probably saying no way, not with all that energy and drive. **The fact is that I was extremely fat, had bright red hair, along with a set of beaver front teeth and I sweated a lot. How's that for attractive?** Oh, and acne was right around the corner, just waiting for me. Did I mention there was a big gap in those beaver teeth too?

MAY 30, 1973

Given all those natural distractions, I did have to deal with an enormous amount of kidding, teasing and all the things that went with that appearance. But for my parents and brothers, you would have thought I was the best looking kid on the block. That's all I needed. I could handle everybody else and it made me almost like superman. I did get into my share of fights over it and won most of them. After all, I was bigger than everybody. Once my peers got to know me, they never saw me as anything but good, big old Tommy, their friend. **Boy, but did those years make me tough.**

Ping Pong Champion — Tommy Lawhead

Let's talk early sports. For some strange reason, I was a hell of a Ping Pong player. I still don't know where that came from, but I could beat the best. I was a lefty. I would have the coaches keeping me after school or ball practice to stay in the gym and play Ping Pong. They could not stand a sixth grader beating them. They would literally get in line to play me. This went on all through middle school.

All four of us were avid swimmers. Again, not sure where that came from because neither of my parents were swimmers. I think my mother got us involved for the competition. I'm not making this up, but my dad bought a membership to a swim club, before he bought our home, when we moved down to South Carolina. Now that conversation went over well, back in Lynchburg, at the dinner table.

Competitive swimming became a huge part of our lives from when we were toddlers through high school. We were members of a neighborhood swim and racquet club where we basically lived from June through August.

Swim team. Wonder which one is Tom?

All four of us were very good chess players, if you count that as sport. The problem was finding others who played. I played church basketball and junior-high football but never much baseball.

The team!

Football was a real eye opener for me. I played left guard most of my career in this sport. Many times I had to play both offense and defense but was assigned as an offensive guard. And believe you me, it was offensive. Man, could we ever stink up a locker room. It was a huge growing experience in terms of character, too. I'll never forget, and neither will my teammates, the time I told the coach I didn't want to do a particular drill because it would really mess up my uniform. I told him my mother had just washed it and I had to try to keep it clean for a while. True story. I don't have to tell how that went over. I still have old school buddies remind me of that day!

Our schools in South Carolina had barely had any integration at this time. I had very little interaction with African Americans, but there was an immediate bond that grew between our races when we began playing sports together. I never really thought about it much until I started writing this chapter. Sports were the one thing that was so easily comingled and universal for us all. Big lesson there. **Look for shared values when building relationships.**

Music, again, kept us somewhat limited to competing in school sports. Nevertheless, the point is that we tried just about everything there was to do growing up. Obstacles were opportunities. A great example was my trying out for the diving team—with my weight. People would chuckle in the stands when I got on the diving board. Well, five years later, I was the diving coach!

Speaking of music, I had my first real band together by the sixth grade. The Soul Syndicate, featuring Big T. You got it: I was Big T. My brother Doug, two years my elder, was the bass player. In the meantime, my two other older brothers, Allen and Mike, were in their own band, called the REGALS. They were very popular, playing all around town, making good money.

Just picture me onstage, in front, as the lead singer, just wailing away out there. **Despite all those physical shortcomings, I was full of confidence and enthusiasm.** The crowds ate it up and so did I.

Are you starting to catch on to my story, *Take this Life and Love it!* I'm not even in high school yet, and I'm worn out recounting the story. How does reading all this help you in life? Read on. There's a whole lot more to cover. We've just started.

Let's try to takeaway something else

9. If you have taken advantage of someone's weakness unfairly, remedy the situation.

10. Take full advantage of all the perks in a job, probably many you don't even realize.

11. If you are a volunteer at some organization or other, never exploit it or take advantage of it.

12. Don't ever let a handicap slow you down.

13. Look for shared values when building relationships.

14. Leadership is a gift. Use it or lose it. Don't waste it. Recognize it. Study it. Learn it. Understand it. Be it! It comes with responsibilities and accountabilities.

15. Whatever you do, try to get involved. Don't sit on the sidelines. Life's too short.

16. Learn how to make money and save it. You'll need it later.

Chapter Three

Do You Ever Wish You Could Do High School Over?

This basically sets the stage for the rest of your life—in most cases. Don't screw it up. There are no instructions and yes, it takes most of us three years to become a senior. Remember, I was the youngest of four Lawhead brothers just entering high school. My three predecessors had already set the stage for me and had left their path of destruction. And with a name like Lawhead, not Smith, it was always great to hear, on the first day of class, "You're not related to those other Lawhead boys, are you?" The rest was history. I had reputations to live up and down to.

By this time in my life I had rid myself of my baby fat and my braces were off and my bright red hair had toned itself down to a brownish red tint. Unfortunately, most of this was negated with my first experience with the much dreaded and feared acne. I was not about to let everyone else have all the fun, so I too did everything possible to promote and grow the cursed emotionally and debilitating disease. I blame the acne mainly on football and sodas.

Yes, I made the team. In high-school football, the more you weighed, the better. It was a smelly, nasty and sweaty experience on the B team, but again, I was going to experience it. You just don't know until you go for it. That was my only year of high-school football, so the next year, I joined the marching band, playing saxophone.

Searching for money again. By this time, I was still playing in the band. My first year of high school was over. For the summer, I got a job with a construction company building a new elementary school nearby. This was my first minimum-wage job. It was as close to hell as you can get and yet, one of the greatest things I ever did. I was quickly introduced to what I knew I was not going to do in life. **Education now had a whole new meaning, meaning it meant everything!** Toward the end of summer I quit the construction job but not before I had an almost life-changing experience.

It was on a late Friday afternoon and I was in one of the buildings under construction, doing my usual menial, disgusting jobs cleaning up the mess the real construction workers would make.

I heard a bunch of guys laughing and cutting up outside the building. They were part of a subcontracting crew that was leaving the job site for good that afternoon. They had finished their job.

All of a sudden they entered my building and started coming after me and I sensed something real bad was about to happen and nobody was going to help. They had been drinking and still had beer bottles in their hands and were making a move to my corner. It was even obvious to me, back then, that this was going to be sexual assault. I could hear them laughing about it and making gross gestures at me.

I didn't scream or freak out but just started running toward the opening in the building as fast as I could. I got out and ran to my car and drove off like a bat out of hell. You could hear the tires screaming. I didn't clock out for the day and drove straight home and closed myself up in my room. **I never said a word to anybody, not even my family, about the incident.** Never mentioned it to the construction foreman and never saw those guys again. Needless to say, God had spared me a horrific ordeal.

When I think about how differently my life might have been had I not gotten away, I start trembling. I hate to even remember that moment in my life, but I can never forget it.

I wanted to get back to doing something to help forget about the whole construction experience. I was lucky enough to get a job as a lifeguard at the swimming pool we belonged to. It didn't hurt, either, that my oldest brother was the manager.

Talk about a change of scenery! I had found my high-school calling. I ended up working all the way through college at this swim and racquet club and having the time of my life. It was truly "loving life!" and getting paid for it.

My last year there, I was the manager, diving coach, swim instructor and lifeguard instructor.

Back to reality. My tenth grade was kind of a holding tank for me. Just stay under the radar and wait to be a junior, and of course, for my acne to disappear.

The band Seal playing for another high school dance

I did start a new band called Seal with five other guys at school. We started playing for all the local dances. My older brothers had moved to the college scene, with a big eight-piece band called Justice. **All three of my brothers were now in that band and making tons of money and meeting lots of nice new friends.**

There was a steak-and-ale restaurant just down the street from our house, so I decided to take a crack at the restaurant business. Once again, **you never know till you've tried it.**

It ranked up there, and I mean "ranked," with the construction business. I was a busboy in an upscale establishment. **The most interesting thing I learned there was how to steal from your employer.** I'm only talking about small things, like cakes and pies, but that's where it starts. A lesson I left there. Oh, and I almost forgot: they taught us how to drink liquor at age 15. **I'll tell you all about liquor later on.** Just keep reading.

Another pretty exciting and unusual adventure, for a tenth grader, was my sailing trip down to Ft. Lauderdale. A buddy of mine, Paul Wagner, in the rock band with me, got us a job helping a university professor and his sister take a 36-foot sailboat from Savannah, Georgia, to Ft. Lauderdale, Florida. For ten days we sailed —well, mostly motored—down the Intracoastal Waterway. It was over-whelming and I was hooked on sailing for life.

Read on and you can hear about all my adult sailing adventures after retiring. More drinking too.

Speaking of alcohol, could this be the answer? I first experimented with alcohol in the eighth grade. No big deal. A few sips of beer at a friend's birthday party and I forgot about it.

I didn't really get cranked up on drinking until I was a junior in high school. Then I began to think what I had discovered was utopia, the answer to everything and a solution for anything. At the time of this epiphany I was being bombarded with testosterone. Girls and booze—what a life! And with all the money I was making and had saved, I was able to take full advantage of both. **These two became a staple of my life. Something that would end up costing me dearly down the road.**

Another life-changing opportunity. My oldest brother, Allen, was starting medical school and was going to have to quit his band, Justice. That was perfect for me, because they had been grooming me to take over when Al left. I just didn't know it would be that soon. He had tried to do both during his first semester in school and found out real fast it was too much. Good news. He later turned out to be one of the premier gynecological oncologists in the country. Good for me and the country!

This was an unbelievable experience for me at my age or for that matter, any age. Here I was in the eleventh grade, traveling all over the Southeast, playing at all kinds of bars, dances and parties and getting paid a small fortune. This would last another ten years. CHING, CHING, CHING!

In my senior year I met a junior who really caught my eye. Five years later, we were married. Read on; it keeps getting deeper.

College SATs? What are they and why is everybody so keyed up about them? My brothers informed me that they were a test you had to take

JUSTICE: Eight piece rock band

to get into college. Great. When and where? That was the last I really thought about it until my day came to take the test. The night before, I was with my band, playing for a Clemson University fraternity party in Clemson, South Carolina.

That morning, I had to drive the band's huge van— because I owned it and rented it to the band—from the gig in Clemson to the University of South Carolina in time to take some silly SAT test. I still don't know what SAT stands for, but luckily, I did well enough to get into school.

Speaking of college, also during my senior year in high school, a good drinking buddy of mine and I spent the beginning of the school year rushing fraternities at the University of South Carolina. Yes, we were still in high school. You're really not supposed to do that.

For those of you who don't know what *rushing* is, let me briefly explain. You spend a week trying to convince a fraternity that you can drink, drink and then drink some more. That's about the gist of it. My buddy and I were so good at it my mother got a call from a member of one of the fraternities congratulating us on being accepted into his fraternity. Well, let's just say that did not sit well with either my mother or the fraternity. She had to explain to the caller that we were just starting our senior year in high school. What a start!

Believe it or not, with all that going on, **I managed to be an honor graduate.**

Carolina, here I come!

Takeaways to Ponder

17. Fortunately or unfortunately, high school usually sets the stage for the rest of your life. Remind your kids of that too.

18. Take full advantage of as many opportunities as you can. You really won't know until you have tried something. Trust me. You may find you love the construction or restaurant business.

19. Stay away from alcohol in high school. And the rest of your life if you can. One wrong split second could change everything in your life and your friend's and family's. Think hard about what you just read.

20. Never steal from your employer.

21. Keep finding ways to make and save money. It can be fun.

Chapter Four

Deciding What to Do with Your Life at Age Eighteen

By the time I got to college I had already done more partying, and so on, than most college graduates. It was not a big deal for me. I had also come from a very large high school, so the size of the campus and number of students didn't intimidate me either.

Let me briefly describe how the whole matter of college was handled in our household:

1. There was never a discussion at my house about whether to go to college or not. Never!

2. There was never a discussion about what college I would be going to.

3. There was never a discussion about what my college major would be.

4. There was never a discussion about where I would live during my college years.

Guys, I'm not making this up. Ask my three older brothers. Here's how it all came down:

We were all going to the University of South Carolina.

We were all going to be premed majors in biology.

We were all going to live at home while going to college.

That was the package deal. Take it; there was no leaving it.

I don't think I've mentioned this yet, but I hated school. Fortunately, for me, it was always relatively easy. I never really studied much, but I did listen in class and took pretty good notes. I always had early morning classes, which I rarely missed, just to get them over with. I mean I hated school. Don't get me wrong. I loved everything about it but the actual schooling.

One of the hardest decisions I ever made was to change majors halfway through school. I had done pretty well in premed. The only problem was that I hated being around blood, sick people and hospitals. Somehow being a doctor made no sense to me. I went to the career office and the different schools of study to look for a major that could fit me for a good job. I looked at education only because I figured I'd get the summers off. I looked at the health sciences because that subject sounded interesting and easy. I never considered law because even back then there were way too many lawyers.

I looked into a music degree, but that would have taken the fun out of music.

I racked my brain trying to figure out what I was going to do and it finally hit me that I was a natural-born businessman. So business school it was. My mother thought I was crazy and my dad said, "Good for you and good luck" and offered to do anything he could to help. **Best decision I ever made regarding education.** I crammed four years of business school into two and finished up on time with pretty good grades. Didn't graduate with honors this time but took away a lifetime of experiences.

Enough about all those boring, life-changing decisions. Let me ramble a little bit about some of my experiences during those brief and blurry college years. I don't think I have mentioned the word *rejection* in this book because it is one thing I never really appreciated and had to learn to deal with early on in life.

Rejection will test your every emotion. **Handling rejection separates winners from losers.** Your ability to deal with rejection will set you light years ahead of your peers. I don't thrive on rejection; I welcome it. It makes me sharpen my game. Anyone can criticize. Think of rejection as recognition.

Let me give you a taste of real rejection. It was on a very hot, muggy, spring afternoon. This happened while we were playing for an outdoor fraternity/sorority party at a high-rise dorm called Bates House at the University of South Carolina. Just the name should have been a clue. That day, we were missing a couple of our regular band members and had some other musicians filling in for them. Big mistake. Long story short: we stunk! After three songs, my brother Mike felt something hit him in the leg. He looked down. It was a chewed up piece of corn on the cob. Next thing we knew, there were tomatoes, hot dogs, onions and pickles being hurled at the band. The more we played, the harder they threw.

Then, to add fuel to the fire, my brother Mike, the comedian he is, shouted over the microphone, "Keep those cards and letters coming." Well, then, all hell broke loose. We ran for the hills. The good news was the students paid us our money anyway but told us to pack our bags and get the hell out and never come back. We went straight to the nearest bar and drank up all our earnings, trying to sort through what had just happened. **I'll never forget that day for as long as I live.** The ultimate rejection for a musician. It took some time to get over it. My confidence took a heavy blow that afternoon.

How many of you would think about ever getting on stage again after that? Well, I did and have been playing ever since. Point is some people would have just given up. Don't. Get over it and make adjustments and charge forward. Think about how many people give up something they love over one bad experience. What a shame and a waste.

Singing with the stars. My drinking buddy from high school was also my drinking buddy in college, Bob Grisso. Bob had become a pretty popular bar tender around town and he also got involved in the entertainment business. He knew a lot of the big bands in our neck of the woods. He especially knew the guys in The Tams and The Drifters, two of the most popular beach bands during our era. I mean they were hot! Still are. Well, he managed to talk both bands into letting us sit in with them at one of their gigs. The Tams let us tag along at a place called Angelo's in Greenwood, South Carolina. It was incredible. During breaks and after the gig, we would get on their bus and start drinking gin, straight out of the bottle, and the rest was history. After that, every time we ran into them playing somewhere, they would let us get onstage and sing a song or two with them. We really thought we were something. It sure didn't hurt our social life either. We ended up doing the same thing with the Drifters at the Thunderbird Hotel in Columbia, South Carolina. Gin again, too! It was something about gin, straight out of a bottle, with a lot of musicians back then. After that, they let us sit in too, anytime we crossed tracks.

Two other big bands I had the privilege of performing with were Otis Day and the Nights and the Cornelius Brothers and Sister Rose. I pulled these off by myself. Sang the last set with Otis in Key West, Florida, in a big, fancy hotel. Remember Otis, "he loves us," *Animal House* fame? He and I both sang the very last song, "Shout," together, with his arm around my neck. I mean he was my hero in college and here I was dipping down with him on "Shout." I was in heaven. Got to go backstage with them too. You guessed it: gin again. Crawled to my room the next morning.

Only sang about four songs with Cornelius Brothers at the Idle Hour Lounge in Myrtle Beach. I didn't know them and they sure didn't know me. I just went up to the stage and asked them to let me sing one of their signature songs, "It's Too Late to Turn Back Now." I knew that song to a tee. Crowd loved it, so they let me sing a couple more songs. No backstage party with them. Don't know what they drank. Never saw them again. Talk about confidence? I was back!

Now you might say singing onstage with these big bands was no great achievement, but for a college kid musician to get this opportunity, **it was the experience of a lifetime.**

Drinking and driving don't mix. Switching gears, no pun intended. Our band, Justice, was playing for a big high-school prom in North Carolina one night and, as usual, most of the band members had gotten pretty sauced. My brother Mike had driven his own car to the gig, but I told him not to drive home. I put him in the band's van and told him to ride with Ricky "Shooter" Ackerman, our keyboard player from Walterboro, South Carolina, and a great guy. I would drive Mike's car home. We all agreed he had had too much to drink and drive.

I started driving out of the parking lot in Mike's beautiful red Mustang, with Vern Mayes, our lead singer. Vern had one hell of a good voice. We were both trying to put an eight-track tape in the tape deck for

Mike's Mustang

the ride home. This high school had a narrow tunnel bridge you had to go through to get out of the campus. To make another long story short, we hadn't gone 500 yards and I crash the car into this stone bridge and totaled the car. I just wasn't looking where I was going. Mike was right behind us in the van, watching his car crunch into the bridge. I think he would have killed me at the time if he had actually realized what had just happened.

One other serious vehicle catastrophe happened on the way to a gig at Clemson University. We had just had the van gassed up and the oil checked and the wheels rotated for the trip. Oh yea, and the cooler was packed neatly to the brim.

Mendel Lindler, our trombone player, was driving and I was riding shotgun. The rest of the van was packed to the brim with musical equipment. As usual, I had just cracked open two Miller beer bottles to get us started on our trip. We hadn't been on the interstate but a few miles, going 70 miles an hour, when all of a sudden we saw a wheel passing us by. Our left rear wheel had literally come off the van and we went crashing into a ditch on the right side of the highway.

To this day, I don't know how Mendel kept us from getting killed. If there had been another vehicle anywhere near us, it would have been all over. We swerved back and forth on the highway until we finally crashed into that deep ditch and cracked the back axle on the van.

Justice's van

We found out later the mechanic had not completely tightened the nuts on the wheel that came off. We were lucky that it was a back wheel and not a front wheel. Otherwise, we would have flipped completely over and neither of us would have lived to talk about it. I still owe Mendel for that one.

Another business opportunity. Every summer during college, I would go to Myrtle Beach for Sun Fun Week. This was always the first week in June. Hundreds of thousands of people would swarm our coast. Each year I would partner up with the main lifeguard who worked right outside one of the most popular hotels on the strand, the Holiday Sands.

Playing on the lifeguard stand out on Myrtle Beach

Every night around midnight I would take my guitar, a quart bottle of Jack Daniels, a six-pack of 24-ounce Schlitz Malt Liquor Bull beer and climb up a 10-foot tall lifeguard stand and start singing and playing. The lifeguard would unlock the beach chairs for people to sit in and gather around for the concert. They would come up and put tips in a big black trash bag at the foot of the stand, which was always handled by one of our girlfriends. We used this method because the wind was always blowing so hard it would sweep away all our dollar bills. The trash bag worked great. Also, they couldn't see how much money we were actually pulling in.

I would split the money 70/30 with the lifeguard. It was worth the 30 percent just to have him keep the cops off our back. The guards always had connections. Unfortunately, I did always have to train and bribe a new lifeguard every year.

While all this was going on, I had **another life-changing experience.** My dad had been taking my brother Doug and me to school in the mornings on his way to work. We would walk down to his office after school and catch a ride home with him. It was a hassle and an inconvenience, but it worked.

One Friday he came by the school to give us a ride home and he had a bunch of boxes in the car. Some of them had pictures of us and the family. My brother asked him what that was all about and you could see him holding back tears.

The company he had worked for, for over 20 years, had let him go that afternoon with no notice or anything. The company had brought in new management and was letting the older guys go and replacing them with much younger ones at much lower wages, something they could never get away with today.

My mother was furious and wanted to sue the company, but my dad just said, "Let's move on." It tore me apart to see my dad broken down like that. This was an overwhelming experience for me. I saw what this company did to a very loyal employee and I saw its lack of respect for human beings. Lesson: Nice guys do get screwed a lot and they need to stand up for themselves. **I vowed from that day on I would never allow a business to have that much control over my destiny.** If anybody was going to do some screwing, it was going to be me. That one day, changed my life forever.

My proud father got back on his feet and struggled to find a job—at his age. It took about six months, but he did get a job and remained at that next company until he retired. Man, what a dad!

While I was going through college I was able to get a job as a page in the South Carolina House of Representatives. A page is basically an errand boy for fat, lazy legislators. But it was a high-profile job and one that was damn hard to get. You had to know somebody to get in. My mother had some connections and got me in on the inside track. I worked at the state house all through college and finished up as a page in the South Carolina Senate for two years.

Now, you talk about an experience. I was there in the thick of the most "good ole boy" politics you have ever seen. Just imagine South Carolina politics in the early eighties. Those from around these parts know it all too well.

Basically, you could count on one hand the men who literally owned and ran the state of South Carolina. And there I was, in the belly of the beast, loving it all and at the same time, sick of it all.

The sad thing is that I was very interested in politics at the time. I had imagined myself a US senator one day. Well, **after almost four years of witnessing some of the most scandalous and crooked dealings behind closed doors, I said no thanks to politics.**

It is really a shame that my early exposure to politics influenced me so negatively that I never wanted to be a part of it. You might ask why I did not get in there and change the system. I knew, even back then, it would take an army to undo that mess. I was not ready to make that sacrifice at that time.

Who knows? Maybe it's time for me to go ruffle some feathers?

Oh, I forgot to mention a few more jobs I took on during college. Every break between semesters I would go down to the local temporary employment agency to pick up some pocket change and beer money and add a few more credentials to my resume.

My favorites were:

- Cleaning out the Carolina Coliseum, from top to bottom, after the Ringling Brothers Barnum and Bailey, week-long Circus Extravaganza—elephant stuff and all!

- Cleaning out the Williams Brice Football Stadium after a Saturday college football game. I think the stadium only held about 70,000 people back then.

- Putting together gas grills for a large retailer. This one still haunts me. I always wonder if I put the darn things together right.

- Sweeping out the Township Auditorium after rock concerts, vomit included, along with beer and liquor bottles, marijuana butts and roach clips.

College, to me, is another one of those make-or-break experiences, in which you develop habits—good and bad—that will last you a life time. You make decisions that could drastically affect your life. Rebounding from bad habits is hard to do.

Takeaways Continued

22. Brainwash your children early on about college. Seriously, make sure it makes sense and is a good investment. A good education is priceless, but college is not for everybody.

23. If you go to college, you will get out of it no more than what you put into it. In other words, try to have some idea of what you want to learn and do when you finish. Sounds simple, duh! Don't let others decide what you want to do.

24. Try to find a job, while in school, in the area of study that you're pursuing. With a prelaw education, for example, get a job at a law firm.

25. If you join a fraternity or sorority, don't make it your major.

26. Start interviewing for jobs no later than the beginning of your last semester.

27. Never let a company own you.

28. Don't drink and drive.

29. Handling rejection separates winners from losers.

Chapter Five

How Can I Spend the Rest of My Life Doing This?

I t is kind of a blur trying to determine when you really are an adult. At least it was for me. Sometimes I wonder if I'm there yet. For the purposes of this book, I'm going to define it by starting with my first real job after college. But before I get there, I need to explain the months up to graduation and my postgraduate months.

I can only remember going on one job interview before I graduated from college. It was with a large Fortune 500 company in a downtown hotel. My marketing professor had recommended me to the recruiter. Well, I got all dressed up and waited in the lobby for about 15 minutes. I got a call that my interviewer was running late, so I wandered into the lounge to wait and ordered a cocktail. Can you believe it? **Let's just say things didn't work out with that interview.** I went straight home where one of my best buddies, Dave Dudley, was anxiously waiting to help me celebrate another lost opportunity. Jack Daniels and coke and two guitars the rest of the afternoon. Better luck next time!

After that, I decided I wanted to work one last summer at the swim and racquet club before getting a real job. That did not go over well with my girlfriend. You see, I had been using college and no job as an excuse to put off marriage. We had been dating for almost five years. This was the last straw for her and we ended up breaking up for a couple of weeks. We did get back together and got engaged. That is a complicated story, for another time.

I did work at the pool until the end of September, but I still was not even trying to find a real job. Somehow, I just knew something would work out. I didn't know how, but I knew it would. I began working part-time at the university and then in January 1982, I landed my first corporate job: adjuster for a third-party collection agency. I really wasn't sure at the time what that meant, but I did know there had been lots of applicants and there were two others starting that day with me.

My first day on the job was spent in orientation and then training. All morning we listened to audio tapes of different adjusters talking to customers about their accounts. I soon found out that an adjuster was just a fancy name for a collector.

Nevertheless, the phone conversations were always pleasant and the customer would graciously agree to the adjuster's demand for payment of a past-due account. Then the manager took us out for a pleasant lunch and we talked about how much fun and how easy this job would be. When we got back to the office, we listened to three more hours of recorded conversations or, I should say, the same crap! By this time I felt sure I had it down and couldn't wait to hit the phones. That would have to wait until the next day.

That night, my in-laws-to-be took my fiancée and me out for an elaborate dinner to celebrate my new job. Boy, was everybody happy and relieved.

The next day finally came and it was show time. Somehow, my first call didn't go quite like the tapes I had heard the day before. I was introduced to words I had never even heard before, along with a lot I knew too well.

This was not a very pleasant old lady on the other end of the phone. She, basically, was threatening my life. After I hung up on her—remember, I'm the collector—I figured it had to be a fluke. So there I go again, dialing for dollars. This call was even worse. The man wanted to talk with my supervisor and threatened to sue me and the company. I began to sweat profusely. Unfortunately, this went on until lunchtime. Not one pleasant phone conversation.

I was in a state of shock. I didn't know what to do, but I had to do something. **How could I spend the rest of my life doing this? Then I thought, how can I spend the rest of the afternoon doing this?** So, for lunch, I went right down the street to a local tavern that also served lunch. I went to the bar and ordered a Jack Daniels and coke along with a hot dog. Thought this might take a little edge off things. Since the first Jack went down so smoothly, I went ahead and ordered a pair to go. Finished one on the way out and the other in the company parking lot.

Here I was back at that phone. It was just staring at me, almost laughing. Things went from bad to hell. All I could think about was getting out of there. What was I going to tell my fiancée and friends? What was I going to say to my new boss?

We were collecting past-due accounts that were three, four and five years in arrears. **There was no way in hell I was trained to collect from these deadbeats.**

Now the fun. How to tell everybody about my second and last day on the job? I can thank old Jack Daniels for giving me the courage to tell my new boss I was quitting. But I sure did miss Jack when I was trying to explain it to everyone else.

Two lessons here. First, I made a mistake with this first job. **I cut my losses early,** although it was very embarrassing. But look at how many people might have just hung in there and been miserable, maybe for years, just to avoid disappointing others.

Second, **never stay in a job that you are miserable in!** I don't care how you do it. Just get the hell out. Anything is better than having a job you hate.

Read on. Things do get better.

I had to finally rely on my father-in-law-to-be to get me an interview with South Carolina National Bank. It was the largest bank in the state at that time. I didn't let my pride get in the way. Another lesson here. **When trying to find a job, you beg for favors and connections to get in front of the hiring line.** I knew this was a job I needed. I was not going to screw this up. I walked into that interview knowing

I was going to convince them to hire me. That was the bar I set. Oh, and of course, my father-in law-to-be helped.

Got the job and the rest is, basically, history. I stayed with the company for the remainder of my first professional career.

Now a lot of things happened during those 17 years.

Where do I start? Well, my first position with the bank was—can you believe it?—that of adjuster—oh, I mean collector—only this time it was credit card collections for mostly good customers, who were occasionally tardy with their monthly payments. Nothing like I had experienced before. Actually, it was challenging but educational and rewarding.

That job proved to be an excellent background for what I would spend most of the rest of my banking career doing: lending money. I am convinced, to this day, that no bank loan officers should be allowed to lend one dime until they have spent some time collecting money that has already been lent. You gain a whole new appreciation for the value of money and how it affects people's lives. This is one unique product: once you sell it, you have to get it back. Think about it. Where else does that happen? Now, I have to give my "abbreviated" soap box speech on the banking industry. Believe me, I could write a whole book on the shortcomings of banks and especially the leadership void.

The day banks started giving bonuses and incentives for the amount of dollars a loan officer would lend in a given year was the downfall of credit quality in our financial institutions. It was literally "the fox in the hen house." Lenders began purposely overlooking obvious short-falls in credit requests just to get the loan through the system and get their bonus.

I saw this coming in the late 1980s in our organization. Then it just took off in the nineties, with very little control. No one loved money more than me, but I knew that tying loan growth to bonuses was a recipe for disaster if not done right. Don't get me started.

Back to my story. I was so good at collecting that I was offered a place in the management trainee program after only five months on the job. This was a major break for me.

The training was excellent, second to none in banking, and lasted over a year. Boy, was I ready to rock and roll. I went through every department in the bank and would literally work in a position there for at least a week or sometimes months, depending on the depart-ment. **I had done almost everyone's job by the time I finished the program.**

My first assignment was to be a commercial loan officer in Greenwood, South Carolina. I really didn't even know where Greenwood was, but I was ready to pack the wife up and go.

Now a commercial loan officer makes loans primarily to businesses as opposed to individuals. Well, in a smaller town, you had to wear all the hats, so I started making loans to anyone who walked into the bank and asked for a loan.

Another big part of my new job was to go out into the community and drum up new business for our bank. I loved this. I was born for this duty and was well trained from my early years as a child salesman, which made others jealous because it was so natural and easy for me.

Oh, I forgot to mention I did marry my high-school sweetheart shortly after starting with the bank. And she courageously agreed to pack up and move with me to this new town.

I guess I should talk a little about my first marriage. We were a great pair. My new boss liked her more than he liked me and she got along with everyone. I could not have asked for a better partner in my early career as well as my young adult life. She went a long way in advancing my position with the bank. **Back then it was very important to have a stable family relationship** and a spouse who supported you. Unfortunately, these days, I really don't think many people or companies care. Another sad situation in our business community.

Enough bragging about her, because I obviously screwed it up. We had been very happily married for almost six years and both careers were going great. She was a dental hygienist and loved her job at the time. We were

Josh Lawhead of Abbeville relaxes in the comfort of his office at South Carolina National Bank. Mr Lawhead and his three brothers form the Lawhead Brothers Band. They will perform at the West ern Foothills United Way United Way dinner Tuesday night

Anderson Independent Mail Monday January 22, 1990

living in Abbeville, South Carolina. It's a small, neat little theater town with plenty of things happening for a small place. And of course, everybody knew everybody's business—Peyton Place Annex.

I was the city executive for the bank, which meant I was really somebody. Big fish, small pond. Her parents and family were great and I still miss them to this day. I couldn't have asked for more from my in-laws. **Lesson: you can pretty much tell what you're getting into, when you are considering marriage, by looking at the parents, especially the mom.** Keep that thought.

She broke the news to me, pretty suddenly, one Monday night at the dinner table in 1988, that she wanted a divorce. Wow! You're kidding. Don't really know if I'll ever know what happened to us, but something did and it must have been my fault. **I agreed to split our assets in half and she moved on.** Probably one of the most uneventful divorces in history. I'm still not sure if we even did it right. It was so simple and painless.

In hindsight I know that I had continually put off having children early in our marriage, because of my job. I also did a lot of entertaining, which kept me out a lot at night, so I figured those things just added up too much and that was that. **Learn from your mistakes.**

I guess I do need to address why I have never had children. It wasn't anything physical, because I never had any issues in that category. I have reconciled myself to the simple fact of my being selfish. That sounds terrible, but I can't come up with another excuse.

Unfortunately, I was so overwhelmed by the ultimate sacrifices my parents had made to raise their four boys, I did not think I was capable of replicating that. Maybe it is a cop-out, but that's how I felt. Maybe more people should give a little more consideration to having babies before they take that leap?

Man, I keep getting sidetracked! Anyway, what was I talking about? Oh yea, careers. This brings up another career takeaway you should write down. I know it probably cost me my marriage, but facts are facts. In my industry, like most, **your first five years at the company determine the rest of your entire life at that company.** I'm not saying that is necessarily fair or right, but that's the way it is. I busted my butt my first years at the bank and it paid off, big time.

After my divorce, life just moved on and in just a few years I was given a once-in-a-lifetime opportunity with the bank to start a whole new division. Remember that hard work I was doing? It was going to be a pilot program to cater to small businesses in the state. I was on my way back to Columbia, where I grew up, to start this operation. Life was great! If I was successful, they would expand the effort throughout the whole bank.

This is when I really made a mark in the banking business. They began using me in media advertisements and on radio as well as hosting socials to introduce our new concept of banking. It was like dream. Like all dreams, we wake up and my wake-up was spelled Wachovia.

Wachovia bought South Carolina National Bank shortly after we had made things a big success with small business banking.

Wachovia's idea and definition of a small business was vastly different from our bank's. Needless to say, Wachovia changed the rules on us in the middle of the game, and we did quite a disservice to thousands of small-business customers. We survived the merger, but things would never be quite the same. My attitude toward management had taken a hit and I just laid low for a while. Disappointment would be

an understatement with regard to the leadership during this transition. A lesson I will never forget.

Several years passed and the bank decided to start another new division called Private Banking. This was not new to the North Carolina Bank, but we did not have it in South Carolina. Once again I was given a unique opportunity to help put this unit together. This was relatively simple compared to what we had done with small business banking. Also, once again, we were very successful in the implementation of this division.

I lasted about three years, dealing with high-end-wealth customers, who were a far cry from my small-business owners. This is when I made my break. It was time for me to call it quits. You see, my problem was that I was an entrepreneurial banker, which is an oxymoron in big banking. Big banks strongly encourage you to leave your thoughts and ideas at home. In hindsight I should have started my own bank as several of my friends did. Who knows? I might have stayed in the business. Glad I didn't!

Let me back up a little and explain how I got to the point of retiring at age 39.

Even before I do that, I need to share another experience in my life that I choose to think very little about now. I call it engagement. Not! I had been happily divorced for almost 10 years when an associate of the bank fixed me up with one of her customers and friends. We hit it off pretty well from the start and knew lots of the same people from high school and so on. To make a long story short, we got engaged after three years of dating. The engagement was entering its second year, if that tells you anything. For the sake of brevity and bad memories, I got frozen feet and ran. **Lesson: Listen to your gut when it growls.** Oh, and don't forget those earlier comments on marriage and parents. If you don't believe me, ask my ex-fiancée's ex-husband. Enough said. Let's move on.

Business Digest

BUSINESS DIGEST OF GREATER COLUMBIA/FEBRUARY 1991

A Bank that Makes House Calls to Small Businesses

by Helen Hutson

Imagine a bank that is willing to adjust its schedule to fit yours—even if it's after 5:00 p.m. Imagine a bank where you always do business with a familiar face. Imagine a bank that understands the problems faced by small business clients and bends over backward to solve them.

According to Tom Lawhead, vice president and manager of the new Business Banking program at South Carolina National Bank, it's all true.

"When we asked small business customers what they wanted in a bank, they answered someone they could do business with on a regular basis. Someone they could get to know. Someone who wouldn't change on them.

"Small business owners want attention from their financial institution," Lawhead said. "When we heard this, we realized we needed to do something special."

> "When we asked small business customers what they wanted in a bank, they answered someone they could do business with on a regular basis. Someone they could get to know. Someone who wouldn't change on them."

In May 1990, South Carolina National Bank introduced Business Banking to the Columbia area. The program is designed for those businesses whose annual revenue is under five million dollars. In South Carolina, that's 85% of the market.

"We're knocking on doors and telling small business owners that South Carolina National is taking an aggressive approach to small business," said Lawhead. "After all, it's the bread and butter of our state."

Business Banking puts the small business owner in a separate category from individual consumers and large corporations. In the past, a small business owner has typically dealt with a corporate banker. But a banker has many

continued

Tom Lawhead's downtown office overlooks some of the small businesses with which his bank's new program will be working.

Getting back to my decision about retirement. My oldest brother, Allen, and I used to talk constantly over the phone about business and how banking and medicine were headed in the same but wrong direction. We would talk for hours about this stuff.

Then he introduced me to the book *Atlas Shrugged* by Ayn Rand. I couldn't put it down. It was only 1200 pages, written in 1957. I was reading about everything I was thinking and experiencing at the time in my career. Now you are either a fan of Ayn Rand or not. No in between. That's all I'll say about that. Go John Galt! Read her book too. It's all about capitalism.

I have to admit, about a year and half before I retired, I knew I was going to get the hell out of the bank. For the sake of not stepping on anyone individually, the bank had no leadership. There was nothing there. North Carolina ran our South Carolina bank and that was it! Case closed. **I had spent my whole adult life studying leadership and found myself not sleeping at night, knowing we were in trouble.**

The real problem with that was the North Carolina bank was losing its leaders too. John Medlin, the chairman of Wachovia, who had literally raised the bank from infancy, was gone and had left at the helm no one capable of leading the bank. It was that, pure and simple. We were lost! It took less than 10 years for the new leadership to destroy the company. In Wachovia's defense, the company may have fared a little better in the 2008 disaster if it had not gotten in bed earlier with First Union. In my opinion, First Union was simply the devil of banking. When I heard about this merger, I should have sold every share of Wachovia I owned, a decision I will regret not taking for the rest of my life. Again, though, it was Wachovia's leadership that allowed this merger to take place.

I watched a magnificent bank crumble in front of my eyes and pocketbook.

I spent that next year and a half preparing for retirement and getting my affairs in order. I had fun just trying to do my job but not killing myself. Remember, I knew I was being released from prison in less than two years and was the warden, parole and probation officer. It was all in my hands, just the way I had planned it. It was a great feeling, but it was scary too.

Now, what in the hell was I going to do for the next 40 years? I'd think of something, I guessed. I knew I could always go back to banking or anything in the financial industry, so I was not worried about security.

Time for Takeaways

30. Don't be afraid of false starts. They help you figure out, where not to go.

31. Marriage. Check out the parents. If it doesn't feel right up front, don't do it, regardless of the situation. Never marry for money or because of a lack of it. Mistakes are too costly. Bottom line: go with your gut. Marriage can be fantastic and I highly recommend it.

32. Divorce. If it happens, get it over with fast and move on. Some things get better with time, but never a divorce! Just take your time the next time you get married.

33. Careers. Your first five years are everything. Make them good.

34. If you're not happy with your job, do something! Make a plan and get it done. You are not chained to your employer. You spend most of your life at work, shouldn't you attempt to find something you enjoy or are good at? Think of what your unhappiness at work does to your family. Repeat: think of what your unhappiness at work does to your family. Take a lesser job, something, anything.

35. Be a leader every chance you get. It makes you stronger, smarter and respected, usually. Leadership comes with enormous responsibility.

Chapter Six

Strategies for Retiring Very Early (11 Lessons on Money)

My last day at the bank was Friday, March 13, 1998. I was officially retired!

Retirement night

A day that will live in infamy. I had planned my whole life around this day. I had no idea that it would come this soon and that I would only be 39 years old. What am I going to do next Monday? Or for that matter, the next 39 years? I took a self-portrait with my camera, smoking a giant cigar and sipping on a "bowl of brandy" that following Sunday night, relishing in the fact that I had nothing to do on Monday. That's how I handled it.

You're probably saying, "Hey, wait a minute. How in the hell did he do that?" Read on and hopefully there will be some significant takeaways in this chapter that will open up some opportunities for you and have you on your way to early retirement.

First you have to commit to the idea of early retirement from the very beginning. When I started at the bank, at age 23, I set a goal of retiring at age 50. There was no rhyme or reason, no strategy or anything, to come up with that age. It was earlier than 65 and sounded better than 55. From that moment on, my life centered on accomplishing my goal. I intentionally bragged to everybody about my goal to self-inflict internal pressure on myself to get it done. It was another way to motivate success. Remember, according to my mother, failure was not an option.

My initial intent in working at the bank was to learn everything I could about money.

1. **How to make it.**

2. **How to save it.**

3. **How to lose it.**

4. **How to invest it.**

5. **How to lend it.**

6. **How to hide it.**

7. How to insure it.

8. How to spend it.

9. How to borrow it.

10. How to give it away.

11. **Very important and little known, how to get to it before age 59 ½ without a 10 percent penalty.**

Once I fully understood all of this, it was my intention to quit the bank and start my own business. I planned to get my business up and running and begin showing positive trends with consistent profitability that were measurable and sell the company within five years. The next step was to repeat step one. Here is my timeline for this to work:

Start work: age 23 (stay for five to seven years to learn steps 1–11)

Start my own business: age 30 (sell in five years)

Start my second business: age 35 (sell in 10 to 15 years)

Start my retirement: age 50

Sounds like a pretty darn good plan, doesn't it?

Well, all that changed after a few years in the real business world. I will elaborate later.

How to make it. First, start with a job at a large reputable company in whatever position is available. Look at the company's reputation, longevity, success, commitment to the community, and so on.

Remember, these are my ideas and opinions and you may not agree with any of them, but they can work.

There are several reasons for this approach, primarily involving benefits. The benefits available to you in a large company are invaluable if you learn to take advantage of all of them. They just don't exist in small companies.

Once you are "inside the company," you begin to make your mark and I mean make it and make it fast. If you have the ambition and desire, you can quickly move yourself up the ladder. **Your first day, month and year will determine your success in that company.** The first five years will determine how much success. There is no turning back after that first day.

Management will begin evaluating you immediately. There is no "break in" period. Every move you make is being watched and graded and evaluated by everyone, especially your peers. Remember the beginning of my book, about my youth, "let the games begin"? This is where all that competition at a very young age paid off.

You basically have to put your job first for the next few years. That means working harder than you physically and mentally think you can.

Do not get involved in work politics or concern yourself with others' affairs. Do not participate or even listen to gossip in or outside the workplace. Try to isolate yourself, while still being available to help others, when needed. Build a reputation as a person people can comfortably confide in and count on for good advice.

Companies are starving for good young leadership. Read everything you can about leadership. Take courses on it. Find great mentors. Immerse yourself in the art of being a leader. Also, read everything you can about motivation and again, take courses on it. You must be a leader to effectively motivate and you must be a motivator to lead.

Once you have obtained much of this knowledge, put it to work. Take every opportunity to get yourself in front of an audience, to talk about the company or a project and begin establishing yourself as an expert on something. It is important to establish yourself as the best at something within your company. Become the **"resident expert."** That will get you on the fast track to move through the ranks. Constantly add to areas of expertise.

Take the opportunity to write articles about something going on in your company or especially the industry or competition. This immediately establishes you as an expert. Become an authority in as many areas as you can. **Never pretend to be an expert or authority in something you are not.** You will lose all credibility. Once again, this just doesn't happen and takes four and five times the effort of your peers.

Step forward. Take advantage of your company's management training program and volunteer to be part of the training when trainees come through the program. Also, volunteer to be part of the interview team for new employees. Companies often use line employees, in addition to human resources officers, to interview candidates.

Consistently and regularly ask your immediate boss for additional responsibilities.

If you position yourself in your company in this fashion, you will make more money than your peers and you will advance faster and create greater opportunities for additional bonuses and incentives.

Now I can just hear it loud and clear, "I've tried all that, and it's just not fair out there! I never get a break." Well, there's your answer. These aren't breaks. Anytime you are not getting ahead, you take inventory of yourself first, and not the company. Most people do the reverse. If you do what I'm preaching and you aren't getting ahead, you need to find another company or department in your company. **The worst thing you can do is stay and be envious, jealous and bitter for not moving up in the company.** There's a problem somewhere and it probably is never *gonna* get fixed.

The last takeaway to make money is probably the best and toughest to pull off. But if you find a way, then you are off to the races, and I mean fast! What is this miracle worker?

Develop a hobby or talent that you enjoy or are just good at that you can make money with, while not interfering with your full-time job. Whoa, now that's a mouth full, I know. Think about this for a while. This could be something you develop during your career or you could be lucky, like me, and already have something.

In my case, it was music. I was able to balance my entertainment career with my professional one. Believe it or not, they even began to complement each other throughout my career. How? My band began playing for my company's various parties throughout the year. When I was playing for other parties, outside the company, I had a tremendous opportunity to network during our breaks. People thought it was terrific that I was an old stiff banker during the week and a talented and fun musician on the weekends. Almost like a Jekyll and Hyde. Being an entertainer gave me the natural ability to be a great networker. They go hand in hand. Once again, it's back to those early roots.

TOM LAWHEAD
"THE MUSIC MAN"

I am not an advocate of attempting two real jobs at once just to earn extra money. This could completely negate everything I've tried to advise you about earlier. I am saying: *look for opportunities that could make sense and not distract from your primary employer.* Like I said earlier, it's not the easiest but one of the best ways to make money.

You see, where this really makes an impact is in savings. I was able to take advantage of all the bank's savings plans because I had the other income to pay regular bills. Also, when it came to buying the larger things a family needs, like a house and a car, I was always able to put more down and get better deals on purchases. You see how all this begins to literally snowball to your advantage?

Now, I have only covered the traditional way of making money and will go into the details of other ways to make money. So keep reading.

How to save it. As soon as your parents are told by the doctor you are on the way, kick them a few times in the womb to let them know you want a minor's savings account started, right away. I'm not kidding. A parent should begin the thought process of **savings for their child the minute that child is born—even before that if possible.** I could draw you tons of illustrations of the effects of this strategy that you would not even believe. But they are true.

There is no substitute for consistent saving and the compounding of those savings for almost guaranteed financial security. Read that again and again and write it on your check book.

I am not a coupon person, but kudos to those who use them. There are thousands of ways to take advantage of saving money when you purchase things, but I am not going to go through a long laundry list. I will try to cover a few larger ticket items to give you some things to think about when making purchases. Before I do that, let me cover the most important thing you can do when it comes to savings.

I'll never forget going through orientation at the bank on my first day at work. I could not believe my ears, when I heard the personnel officer explain that for every dollar I saved in the bank's retirement plan, the bank would match 100 percent of that, up to 6 percent of my salary. I made her repeat that several times to me to make sure I heard it right. She agreed it was a great benefit, but very few took full advantage of it. I told her to put me down for the max immediately and to increase it if the bank ever offered more. She just laughed and said okay.

Seventeen years later at the bank, I was saving 15 percent (the max at that time) of my pretaxed income and the bank was still matching 6 percent. That meant I was saving 21 percent of my total salary every week. I don't even need to go through the math to give you some idea of how fast that grew. It was almost like stealing. Still, many employees only took advantage of a portion of this benefit. Maybe that second home or fancy car just didn't leave much extra to save?

Another huge benefit employees fail to grasp is the power of pretax investing and saving. **If there were one thing that I could wish for every one of my readers, it would be to have you educate yourself and be able to fully understand the enormous value of pretax investing and pretax compounding,** enough already.

Homes. I was fortunate that my company had a very good relocation package, so I usually did quite well when moving with the bank.

Since I was a banker, I had a pretty good knowledge of how real estate transactions were handled. I usually tried to buy a home directly from a seller, to avoid realtor fees and other costs with third party sellers. If I did work through a realtor, I would always try to negotiate a reduced fee with the seller or try to get the seller to absorb some of the cost. **If you don't ask you won't get it.**

When it came to getting an attorney, appraiser, inspector, and so on, I would always try to use one of my customers first. After that, I would ask friends for good referrals. I did some bartering also, with my music. I would offer the band's services for a party, or some occasion down the road, in return for services.

Have your financing in place, long before you make an offer on a house. This puts you way ahead of other potential buyers and gives you much stronger negotiating power over price. This is easily done by going to your bank and getting the loan preapproved upon certain conditions.

Never buy a house without an absolutely thorough inspection! I mean thorough. And by someone you know and can rely on, not someone referred by the selling party. I think it is almost as important as the appraisal. Talk about saving money. If you miss something on the inspection and find problems after the closing, you are in a mess. Pay a premium for a good home inspection.

When you are ready to sell your home, always try to sell it yourself first. A lot of people will disagree with me on this, but I stand by my advice. Now there are plenty of circumstances where this just can't apply.

I'm talking about someone who will spend the time and effort to do market research, fixing up, repairs, marketing, and so on. If you are not willing to put lots of effort into it, hire a realtor on the front end and try to negotiate the fee.

Automobiles and boats. Get to know a dealer and build a relationship with that person long before you are ready to buy something. It's great if the dealer is a neighbor or customer of yours. Try to avoid trading in your car. Sell it yourself. Nine times out of ten, you will make more money. Again, these seem like hassles and unimportant, but you must want to retire early if you are still reading my book. This is how it is done. Try to pay cash for autos and boats because they are rapidly depreciating assets. I don't even consider them assets. I think of them as liabilities from the start. At the very minimum, insist on great financing terms and put some money down. **Never, never buy more car or boat than you can afford!**

Once you have saved it, in pretax dollars, never spend it. What I mean by this is **never tap into your retirement savings for anything other than retirement.** You're already saying, "What about emergencies?" Yes, they will come up. If you need money for an emergency, you should consider borrowing it before you dip into pretax savings. Yes, borrow first. That's how important the compounding of pretax money is!

A reminder. Pretax dollars are monies you save in 401k, IRAs, and so on, **that are not taxed** when you invest them. When you cash these in, before retirement, you are not only taxed and penalized, but more important, their value immediately is lost because of the additional savings that accrue when monies are not being taxed and are continually compounding. It is almost impossible to calculate exactly how much you end up losing by tapping those savings early. That's not the smoothest way to put it, but trust me. Try to save as much money that is not taxed as you can. **Never give the government any money sooner than you have to.** Now, does that make it clearer?

Second home. There goes early retirement. Enough said.

How to lose it. Most of you are probably already experts at this. I'll try not to hurt anyone's feelings or embarrass you as I list some of my favorite ways of losing it. This does not apply to using a professional, qualified, financial advisor.

- Take a friend's stock investment advice.

- Take a stranger's stock tip/insider trading advice.

- Gamble.

- Invest in something you know nothing about.

- Amateur day stock trader or hedge fund trader.

- Bad record keeping.

- Avoidable fees.

- Pay too much for something you just have to have.

- **Lending to family and friends (I'll cover this later).**

- Hiding cash and forgetting where you put it. (Laugh, but it happens!)

- Drink alcohol excessively and/or do illegal drugs.

- Lawsuits.

- Bad health habits causing avoidable medical expenses.

I bet you could give me a heck of a lot more, but these really hit home for some of us. Just remember how hard it was to make the money you are getting ready to risk for the wrong reasons.

How to invest it. Most of my life, I did my own investing. That was because of my background and knowledge and homework, I committed to understanding the stock market. I just recently turned all that over to a professional financial advisor and am very happy and relieved to no longer be handling the account. Don't get me wrong. I'm still reviewing my monthly returns.

I think deep down the best advice I would give 90 percent of my readers is to **let a professional take responsibility to invest your money wisely,** based on your expectations and wants. I know I seem to be always advising ways to save and cut corners, but this is another one of those areas you don't skimp.

You need to do some major shopping for a well-known, qualified, successful, financial planner, who has all the credentials and licenses to manage investment funds. This is one of the most important decisions you will make in a lifetime. Make it a good one. Most planners will charge an annual fee of at least 1 percent of the total savings they manage, and it is well worth the expense.

I strongly advise people to not invest in the family's or friends' businesses. Boy, I know I'll catch hell on this one. Let me try to put it another way. If you do, go in understanding, this is a gift, not an investment and you don't expect them to pay you back and you can afford that. If you do get it back, great!

It's just not a very pretty situation when things go bad, and in many cases they do. I know there are circumstances where family is the only source of capital. If you do invest, get involved and understand daily what your investment is doing. Again, if you are not directly involved in the venture, encourage your family or friend to first seek conventional financing.

How to lend it. Don't! It's that simple. You are not a bank and don't want to be one. This is one of the stupidest things an individual can do, period! I have spent my entire professional adult life lending money. I have lent hundreds of millions of dollars over my career. It's a good thing I was pretty darn good at it. If you want to lend money, go get a job at a bank and lend the bank's money. I'm not kidding about this one. Unless you have been professionally trained and have experience lending, just say no to any request. The same rule applies here as it does in investing when it comes to family and friends. Avoid it and find other alternatives.

If my brothers had ever asked me for money, which they never have, I would gladly give them what they needed if I could afford to. But I would never consider it a loan. That's how you keep a brother or sister. I know they would pay me back, but I'm already conceding they can't.

How to hide it. IRS 101! Learn the tax system if you have the time or interest. None of us do, so:

Pay handsomely for a great tax advisor. This will be one of the best investments you ever make.

It is impossible for individuals to do themselves justice by filing their own tax return.

One other crazy piece of advice is to literally hide it. You thought I was joking earlier about people losing money they hid. I'm actually talking about putting some cash in a safe deposit box at the bank. I recommend having at least several thousand dollars in cash that you could put your hands on in an emergency. Put it there and leave it there. If you take some out, replace it as soon as you can. **Cash is and always will be king.**

How to insure it. I covered earlier ways to lose your money. This is where we will discuss how to protect yourself against some of those situations and some other ideas about looking out for your money.

Liability insurance is probably one of the most important instruments you will need to protect yourself against all types of situations. Here is a list of almost mandatory insurance products:

Liability. You need this for property, vehicles, boats, and so on. Depending on your profession, you may need significant coverage for protection against law suits.

Life. Have enough to cover all your liabilities. Also, enough to sustain the lifestyle of all your immediate surviving family. Term life is more economical and I would recommend it. If your company provides it, take advantage of the low premiums most companies offer. If your spouse works, secure an amount for each of you, according to how much each of you contributes to household income.

Disability. I am not that much of a fan of this, probably because I have not studied it as much as other types of insurance. This obviously has a lot to do with your profession and the danger or risk in your occupation.

Health. Make sure you have at least enough coverage to handle catastrophic situations. I advise higher deductibles.

Long-term care. Expensive. This is definitely a personal decision and preference and I hesitate to give an opinion because it is so sensitive.

Insurance is another financial area where you truly need a trusted professional to review and keep you adequately secure to avoid disasters. You need to protect what you have worked so hard for and could lose overnight if not insured sufficiently.

How to spend it. This follows closely from how to lose it, except everybody is an expert on this one. I wish we could all just say, "Use common sense," but that ain't *gonna* fly. About the only light I can shed on this one is to always remember what it took to earn the money, and is what you're buying worth that much? Now, wasn't that easy?

How to borrow it. My background as a lender all my life has made me even more of an expert in borrowing money. I already know exactly what it is going to take to get the financing I need.

Do your homework before you approach a bank to borrow money. A bank is the first place to normally secure a loan.

Never just walk into a bank and apply for a loan. First, try to establish a relationship with a banker, not a bank. As soon as you open an account, find out who the manager is and introduce yourself. Make a habit of saying hello to that person when you go to deposit money or withdraw. Let the manager get to know you personally. Try to get on a social level with him or her, if possible.

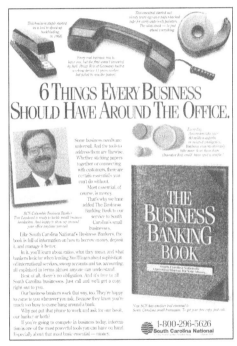

Tom developed the idea and helped create a simple book, for the bank, to help customers understand banking.

When the time comes to borrow, have all you need and then some, as it relates to your financial history. **Overwhelm the bank with your excellent organization of data.** Have your facts together and your request clear and understandable. Have any and all supporting documentation related to what you are using the money for and most important, the documentation to show your ability to repay the loan. I know this sounds simple, but nobody does it. Trust me, I've been there.

You would be shocked at the power your presentation has over how you are taken care of by that banker. Now that might sound discriminatory, but that is just the way it works. So now that you know that, you don't have any excuses.

Don't hesitate to ask for better terms if you feel you warrant them, or that you could do better somewhere else. Just be courteous and not threatening in your request.

How to give it away. Philanthropy. What would we do without it? Even when it hurts, try to give to God. Other than that, I would look to organizations that have assisted you or your family in the past, ones that you have a passion for. Always consider organizations that you can directly feel assisting your community. **Accountability is important when giving to charity.** Do your due diligence when contributing.

Very important and little known: how to get to it before age 59 ½ without a 10 percent penalty:

Get a pen and paper and take notes.

What I am about to explain is somewhat complicated and will need the assistance of a good banker and/or financial advisor but can be done without the cost of an accountant or CPA if you study the rules and deal with a reputable financial institution.

Remember the term *rule 72(t)*.

Basic definition: an Internal Revenue Service (IRS) rule that allows for penalty-free withdrawals from an IRA account. The rule requires that in order for the IRA owner to take penalty-free early withdrawals, he or she must take at least five "substantially equal periodic payments" (SEPPs). The amount depends on the IRA owner's life expectancy calculated with various IRS-approved methods.

Now, get to it!

Seriously, this is a little known avenue to tap into your IRA prior to 59 ½ without the 10 percent penalty and is completely legal without major catches.

I have been taking equal distributions for over ten years from my IRA and basically, living quite comfortably. I still pay ordinary income on the distribution, but with no other earned income, my tax is minimal.

My investments have been exceeding my withdrawals, so I'm set for life.

Well, I was, until 2008. That has been a bump in the road, but as I described earlier, things have been turning back around. I continue to take my same quarterly distributions and the account should still outlast me.

The obvious **key to this strategy is to have accumulated a pretty good sum in your 401k, early on.** Remember my savings strategy. It's for a reason.

IRS revenue ruling 2002-62 provides guidance on how the payments can be determined. There are actually three different methods you can use.

1. The required minimum distribution method. Take the balance in the retirement account and divide it by the life expectancy. The annual payment is calculated each year.

2. The amortization method. The balance in the account is divided by a specified number of years according to a life expectancy and multiplied by an interest rate that is not more than 120 percent of the federal midterm rate. The annual payment stays the same in future years.

3. The annuitization method. This method uses the account balance, an annuity factor based on a mortality table, and an interest rate. The annual payment in future years also remains the same under this method.

There are resources and calculators, such as Bankrate, to calculate your maximum distribution according to the 72(t) exception and the effect the distribution would have on your retirement account balance.

All of these methods can be distributed monthly, quarterly or annually.

Your financial advisor can walk you through this process.

As I said previously, it has been working for me for over ten years without any problems.

Oh, and I almost forgot: some states allow a tax deduction for these withdrawals.

How About Some More Takeaways?

36. There are at least seven financial experts you need to develop long-term relationships with and be willing to pay handsomely for their advice. All the money you invest in these individuals will almost always be well worth every penny provided you find the right people.

    Do your homework and due diligence when selecting each one. It scares me to death when some of my friends confide in me on how they decide to hire or retain experts for such mammoth responsibilities and accountabilities. I think some of them spend more time deciding what clothes to wear to a cocktail party.

    These financial experts are:

    financial advisor (well licensed)

    CPA (certified public accountant)

    lawyer (a general lawyer) and always use a lawyer well qualified in the matter you are needing a lawyer for), not necessarily your general lawyer

    local branch banker (for every-day banking needs)

    insurance agent (experienced, reputable company)

    real estate agent (you never know when or why)

37. Never stop saving money until you retire. Don't look for an excuse.

38. Learn my 11 lessons on money.

39. Career. Put all your energy, effort and time into the very beginning of the game. Don't save up for the second half. It may never come.

40. If you are not constantly growing in your job, make something happen. Don't wait. Just do it.

41. Don't be afraid to retire early. I know you're out there.

Chapter Seven

There's Never a Bad Day
on the Lake Fishing

I t's Monday, March 16, 1998. I don't have a job. I don't have any
plans. All my friends are at work. There is nobody to play with.

I've never been happier in my life.

Blame it again on *Atlas Shrugged* by Ayn Rand. I read this book over
and over for a period of about six months. The more I read, the more
I realized I was experiencing exactly what this book was all about.
Capitalism, leadership and all the things I lived for and trained for
were being destroyed, not to mention that **by the time I added up
all the taxes I was paying, the government was basically my 50/50
partner** in life. In other words, the government was taking half of
everything I earned. That just ain't right.

To make matters worse. Don't get me started. **The government
was taking half my income and literally paying the bills for over
50 percent of the population that pay no tax.** Now, let me get

this straight. Somebody out there is living off my salary and doing nothing. Something is drastically wrong.

It will never change or get better until people start taking accountability for themselves. Once you start sucking everything from the "providers" (that's you and me), we will eventually say enough is enough. There is nothing good about the government providing everything for anyone.

I better stop here on that subject.

What do I do now? For the next year I found myself engulfed in pleasure and gratification. There was so much to do. I couldn't figure out how I ever worked and got everything done.

During this time, I was getting calls from friends and associates asking if I had lost my mind and when I was going back to work. It was always, "You're too damn young to retire!"

There were plenty of job offers, but I was not the least bit interested. I was retired and very happy. The best part was that all those years of saving and investing made it possible to play hard and not worry about the financial impact of not working. **Worst thing you can do is retire and worry about every penny you spend.** It ruins your best years and defeats the purpose of retiring. Also, don't be embarrassed about retiring early. I had a problem with this early on. I got tired of everybody saying, "You're too young to retire," so I started saying I was unemployed. Brag about it!

Finally, I broke down and went back to work to help a friend out. I agreed to help put together a new marketing effort for the financial company he was president of, and then move on. That took a year and I was back on the streets.

Relaxing at one of many marinas, after another adventurous journey.

This time, I took off sailing for a couple of years. I had a good friend, Duncan MaCrae, who owned a 48-foot Juneau sailboat and was always needing some extra crew to sail up and down the East Coast. He and his brother Scotty also owned a very popular restaurant and tavern in Columbia, South Carolina, called Yesterdays. Pat Conroy, the famous author from our state, has mentioned Duncan's restaurant in his books. That's how famous it is.

Now, I was having some serious fun and good times. This was truly "taking this life and loving it!" at its best.

Then comes another near-death experience. We were sailing from Charleston, South Carolina, to Ft. Lauderdale, Florida, for the annual boat show at Bahia Mar Marina—me, Duncan

Tom, Al, Chip and Duncan, celebrating a successful voyage up the entire east coast.

and his best friend from Kennebunkport, Maine, Chip Malik and his buddy Al. Now, all these guys were Vietnam veteran marine helicopter pilots. That's a crew you want on board with you anytime, anywhere. Oh, and they knew how to have fun too.

We were over a hundred miles offshore from Daytona Beach on our way south. Everything had been going along great so far on our trip. We were ahead of schedule and having a blast. Out of nowhere we started hitting some rough water and heavy winds. This was around midnight and the visibility had gone to almost zero. I remember my shift at the wheel was coming up. We took three hour shifts at the wheel and three hour shifts before the wheel, backing up the captain. So you were basically at the wheel for six hours at a time. I had been watching for three hours, so I was up to take the helm. By this time we were in 15-foot seas. That is not good for the size of boat we were on and pretty damn dangerous and scary. The boat started taking on water and there was nothing we could do about it. The wind and seas just kept hammering us and getting worse. By the end of my three hours the seas were over 20 feet and nothing was letting up. I have never been so afraid in my life. Nobody on the boat was talking. I think we all knew something bad was about to happen. There was no way we could sustain the hits the boat was taking.

Duncan was up next and took over for me. I crawled down in my cabin and stripped naked. I was freezing, but I didn't care. I was literally numb all over. I was shaking and wanted to start screaming and crying. All I could think was this was the end and what a stinking way to go.

I remember huddling up in the corner of my bunk in a fetal position and just thinking about what it was going to be like to drown. I loved the ocean. I loved the lake and the river. I had spent my whole life around water. I just never imagined it taking my life.

After about 15 minutes at the wheel, Duncan made the decision to turn the boat toward land and try to creep to shore. Remember, we were over a hundred miles from land, in a sailboat. Turning into the shore had plenty of risk and could tip the boat over.

It was pitch dark. Nobody could see anything. Waves were crashing over the bow of the boat and washing all the way over the back of the boat. We were not going to make it. After a while, I just calmly drifted off to sleep. I had come to peace with the fact that I probably would never wake up again. Man, that was a weird feeling, but that's how it worked.

When I did wake up, we had weathered the storm and were nearing land.

Nobody on that boat ever showed any fear to the others during the storm, but all admitted later we never thought we would make it.

We ended up in Ponce Inlet, Florida. Never heard of it before and don't remember much about it. You see, as soon as we hit land, we started drinking and didn't quit until the bartender and his friends carried us off to some old cabins nearby to sleep it off.

When we all finally sobered up, we were back off to the Ft. Lauderdale boat show. Our buddy Chip bought a beautiful 36-foot Sea Ray boat. We drove it all the way up the Intracoastal Waterway to his place at Kennebunkport, Maine. Two weeks on the water. Another indescribable adventure.

Tom wishing he was down in the hull drinking rum with the rest of the crew

The next chance I got to go sailing after that was with Dennis Conner, three-time America's Cup winner. For those of you who don't know much about sailing, he was the ultimate sailor in the world. What a once-in-a-lifetime experience for me. I was lucky enough to be invited by Merrill Lynch Investments to a huge fundraiser for the America's Cup. I think I might have exaggerated my net worth on my financial statement to get my invitation. Nevertheless, I had lunch with Dennis and then went sailing in the Charleston Harbor with him. Damn, that was awesome!

Enough about all this sailing and water. It's time for me to stay on dry land for a while.

Another call came for an opportunity too good to turn down. Again, I was not looking or wanting any part of this, but it just happened. Transamerica Business Capital needed a regional manager to work from home and be responsible for making US Small Business Administration Loans for North Carolina, South Carolina and Georgia.

This was something I was good at and had much experience with. The salary was more than I ever made at the bank and more important, it was my first effort at a home-based business. I **learned everything I needed to know about running a business from my home.** That proved to be invaluable down the road. Transamerica did things right and taught me some very valuable things. It was just another terrific professional experience for me.

Tom in the office/ man cave

That lasted a year. Then the company closed the division and I was given a huge severance package. No complaints on that adventure. Give me another one of those, anytime!

Tom aboard "Frangines" docked at St. Thomas, VI

It was obvious I needed to get back on the water before I got my hands dirty again, and so off I went. This time it was off to the US Virgin Islands. Now there's a place I could really retire. I think this is where my liver started having some second thoughts. I'll get back to that thought later.

Taking a 55-foot catamaran from Charleston, South Carolina, to St. Thomas, US Virgin Islands, is a trip everyone should experience.

It takes a few months to get over trips like that. Maybe even years, now that I think about it.

I'm starting to lose track of my time line here, but I'm pretty sure quite a few years have sneaked by.

Let me back up a few years and describe how I started my own company, after Transamerica. Remember, they taught me all the ins and outs of running my own little shop.

The Hunter Group, Business Advisors, was formed by me. I was the company. It was and still is a sole proprietorship. I guess for the last 10 years or so I have helped primarily old, former customers and associates with all sorts of financial needs. I'm kind of a jack of all trades, so to speak.

This is a nice little venture that provides some play money and pocket change. It also keeps me in the loop of business and finance.

My business card says I handle—Hang on. I have to go get one and look at it, again. Oh yea, business finance, mergers, acquisitions liquidations and business sales. My biggest problem now is I ended up helping old friends and never charging anything. Well, what are friends for anyway?

It's September 2003 and the day I have dreaded my whole adult life comes. **My father dies.** He had been sick for about a year and was 81 years old. He finally just wore down. He had several health issues, but for the most part was healthy until his last year of life.

I had the greatest opportunity, the last few years of his life, to become even closer to him than ever before. We were best friends and it was the most fascinating and educational time of my life. We would sit around his house while my mother was watching the soaps, and sip on vodka, telling stories and playing guitar and singing. I could just listen to him talk forever. He was just a damn smart man.

Pap with his Cromwell guitar

It brings tears to my eyes just to think about it. But what a chance of a lifetime. How many sons get the opportunity that I did and took full advantage of? Now that's how to take this life and love it. **Man, you just don't know what you're missing** if you don't grasp an opportunity like that. I miss him dearly, but I had so much quality time with him I can't help but get motivated, not sad, when I think about him. Now that's the way I think it's supposed to be.

It was a beautiful funeral and celebration of life. I sang at it. I don't know how, but God got me through it.

Next adventure? I took a stab at the investment banking business. This is mergers and acquisitions of companies and the financing of those companies, the most complicated and difficult industry and profession around. You earn your money in this business! I call it elephant hunting. You work on a particular deal for months, usually years, before something gets done. You either end up making a whole lot of money on a relationship or you earn nothing. I learned more about business and negotiating than I could imagine possible—once again, a fabulous professional adventure.

I was fortunate to work with a group called the Capital Corporation, out of Greenville, South Carolina. Great experience and great people!

I ought to be getting pretty darn smart by now.

Starting to lose track of time again.

By now I'm living on a big lake with a fantastic view of the water, so I figure it's time to take up striper fishing. Just my luck. One of my neighbors, who owns pawn shops, used to be a fishing guide. Now how good is that? For those of you who don't know, it takes a long time to be a good striper fisherman. I had just cut my learning curve down to nothing.

My new best buddy, Jim Barber, and I are still fishing together at least once a week. That started about 10 years ago. There's nothing like getting up at four in the morning to get started to go do nothing but

Striper season

fish. And man do we fish. **Never a bad day on the lake fishing.** It's just impossible. I don't care what goes wrong, how bad the weather is, and it still ends up being a great day on the water. Ladies, I know that makes no sense.

I forgot to mention I have a 350-pound marlin and a 100-pound sailfish on my wall at the lake. I caught those in the ocean.

There's a lot more I guess I could say about the past 10 years, but a lot of it might not be too suitable for many.

I will add that all during all this time **I have kept the music going and I'm playing every chance I can.** I

Marlin and Sail Fish

can't count the wedding receptions, proms, college and anniversary parties I've played for. I've also been singing at dozens of weddings and am starting to do funerals now.

During all these 40+ years as a professional musician, I have managed to accumulate quite an inventory of musical instruments. My lovely wife, Diane, is about at her limit on my toys.

Here's a quick glance at some of my collection:

52 guitars

2 trumpets

48 microphones

15 harmonicas

3 mandolins

1 portable grand piano

2 banjos

3 complete PA systems

1 upright bass (it's big)

5 guitar amplifiers

1 cello

2 trombones

5 saxophones

2 flutes

4 clarinets

4 violins

space is running out!

Takeaways from Paradise Island

42. Set up an office in your house, whether you have your own business or not. It's a good way to get you started should you decide to become an entrepreneur. It is just a must and great to have. It can be an organizational heaven if you set it up right.

43. Tax advantages in having a little side business and a home office.

44. Please make the effort to spend quality time with your aging parents. I mean physical visits, not just a weekly phone call. You will never regret this.

45. At some point in your life, take the opportunity to go sailing in the ocean. Now that's something you'll never forget or regret. Trust me again on this one.

46. Learn to play a musical instrument early in life. At least pick one up when you retire. It really is hard to explain to a nonmusician the pleasure, value and just plain fun of playing and singing.

Chapter Eight

Dodging Death: My Near-Death Experience

L et's just say 2008, 2009 and 2010 didn't go so well. You can also say they were the worst of times and ended up being the best of times. Lots of things happened. These were truly defining moments in my life. A challenging time that covered a lot of people, places and emotions. I sometimes think about all those wonderful years growing up with almost no worries and happiness all around. I want that again.

Let's start with 2008 when I had over half my life's savings stolen from me by the very bank I worked for my entire adult life, The stock went from $65 a share to almost nothing overnight. The criminals at the bank had made terrible loans and withheld all kinds of financial information from analysts in order to keep the shareholders in the dark.

This wasn't just a few bad apples; it was institutional fraud and nobody got punished. Just the opposite. All the crooked bankers walked away billionaires!

I foolishly had much of my retirement money invested in the bank stock. At the time, the bank was considered the third best-run bank in the country and was over 150 years old. How could anything go wrong? And if it did, surely the stock rating companies would give us plenty of warning? Only problem is they were in on the criminal activity too.

I was experiencing a reverse of the Old West. Instead of the robbers robbing the stagecoach and travelers, the stagecoach was robbing the travelers. The big difference back then was the thieves were shot when they got caught. Now, they were being given huge parachutes full of money and perks.

Does it sound like I'm bitter? You're damn straight I'm bitter! The sad part of the whole thing is that millions of people were robbed in 2008 by crooked bankers and they damaged so many lives and families. We will never see a penny of all this money the big banks are supposedly paying in penalties and fines. Big lesson here: **Don't put too many eggs in any basket,** even if it seems you could never lose anything.

This took its toll on me financially, mentally, physically and spiritually. I'm not kidding! Keep reading.

Financially. How was I going to replace all this money that was stolen from my retirement account? It wasn't a matter of just waiting for the stock price to go back up, because the bank gave itself away to another bank for almost nothing. My stock was basically worthless. All I could think about were the billions of dollars these people took from average people depending on this money for retirement.

I had to just sit back and settle myself down and completely reevaluate my financial situation. Now, every decision I made concerning money I had to think twice about. I had been financially set for life before this disaster, all because of what I thought was sound financial planning.

Back to the drawing board. I immediately cashed in my pension plan on my fiftieth birthday. This is money some companies contribute to their employees for their retirement. It was still intact and a nice little sum. In other words, it was a great windfall for me. I took that money and aggressively invested it in the stock market to help offset my losses. It worked! Took about five years, but I managed to replace a good bit of what was stolen. I'm still pretty bitter.

Mentally. Every time I went to buy something or thought about my bills, I would think I shouldn't have had to worry about this. It was just not fair! What I could have done with all that money! Get over it!

Physically. We are still in 2008, on my fiftieth birthday. My girlfriend, Diane, had reserved us a beautiful place in the North Carolina mountains for a getaway. It sounded great. Only problem was the morning after my birthday, **I went into a massive seizure and almost died.**

I was ambulanced to the nearest hospital and stayed for a week, doing tests. We still don't know for sure what the actual cause was, but we think it was from alcohol withdrawal. I was in perfect health and had not been to a doctor in years. The last time I was in a hospital bed was when I was born.

I just decided to stop drinking, cold turkey, for six months, to see if that was my problem and to see if I could. By that time I had started drinking more alcohol than I ever had in my life. And I was drinking pretty hard before all the financial mess.

Spiritual. This is when I began my spiritual journey that would end three years later, being reborn as a Christian and saving my life.

After six months had passed, I started drinking again. I was generally assuming there was no physical problem and certainly no drinking problem or abuse, since I was able to quit for a while.

Well, I was wrong and I was drinking too much and I knew it. I wasn't harming anybody, but I needed to do something. I began asking God to help me with my situation. I prayed pretty regularly for a solution that would not result in some catastrophic event, like a car wreck or something. I did not want to have to reach bottom to rise again.

I prayed to God about how drinking was such a part of my personality that I could not imagine functioning in public without it. Man, that was sad. I knew that I would not be able to handle it if I were to severely harm someone or cause a fatal accident due to drinking.

Well, life just kept on trucking along as usual with no major hiccups or changes. I was still the life of the party but always worrying something could happen. **It was Russian roulette, each night.**

I would wake up in the middle of the night in cold sweats, dreaming I had done something terrible. It was so real and when I realized it was just a nightmare, I would almost cry myself back to sleep.

Then something happened on my mother's eighty-fifth birthday. The plan was to all meet at this fancy restaurant to celebrate the event. There was just one problem for me. I could not get any of my clothes to fit me that night while I was getting dressed. It was just plain weird. I didn't freak out, but I was concerned. I felt okay. I had pulled two hernias the week before, so I thought that might have something to do with it. I had not been to the doctor about the hernias and really didn't know what they would cause or harm.

I finally dug up an old pair of pants that came close to fitting but still wouldn't buckle. I had to just rig myself into an outfit. No way was my shirt going to button, so I left the tie loose. I was starting to get a little scared.

When we got to the restaurant, everyone was already there. I was sitting next to my brother Allen, the oncologist, and explained my unusual situation. He felt all over my body and kept rubbing my belly. After about 10 minutes he looked at me and very calmly said, **you have ascites.** Then he called my brother Mike, the urgent care doctor, to look at me. He felt all over and also knew right away it was ascites.

Well, I didn't know what in the hell that was, but they were pretty concerned and set me up immediately with a good friend and great internist, Dr. Jerry Robinson. I had gained 25 pounds overnight. My liver had just stopped functioning and shut down. All my fluids were just pouring into my abdomen.

Long story short: I had severe liver and esophagus damage and was about to die.

I was diagnosed with:

- cirrhosis of the liver
- esophageal avarices with esophagitis
- esophageal stricture
- anemia
- acute alcohol hepatitis
- gastroparesis
- hypercholesterolemia
- tachycardia
- cholestatic jaundice

If I did not stop drinking immediately, I would die within months.

God had given me his answer. It was perfect. The only one who was directly hurt and suffering was me. That's not to say others were not devastated by the news, but it was news that I could handle and so could they.

I did not have a choice going forward. At least, I did not think so. I had way too much to live for and more important, my family was counting on me to get well.

What a solution to my drinking problem, and I prayed for it. Instead of being upset and depressed, I was relieved. Yes, relieved was the sensation I had. I knew that if I had kept on going the way I was, something terrible was going to happen. I had dodged my share of bullets and my time was running out.

I prayed, prayed and prayed to God, thanking him for my cirrhosis. During the year following my diagnosis, I never remember once asking God to heal me. That sounds crazy, but I knew it was up to me to make the decision to live or die. It was simple. Listen to the doctor, take my medication and never drink alcohol again for the rest of my life. Now it was up to me to decide my fate.

Now, it wasn't a cake walk, getting well and those first few months were a little touch and go. At the very beginning they considered a liver transplant and were preparing me for the donor list.

On October 7, 2011, I was diagnosed with the disease. On the morning of January 26, 2012, **I met with my minister**, Dr. Tim Philips of Riverland Hills Baptist Church, to discuss what I had been through and my spiritual situation. It was a life-changing morning. He very bluntly put things in perspective for me as to what it means to be a Christian. I realized that day I was an almost Christian. A Christian wanna-be. The definition of an almost Christian is one who is always doing good, gets along with everyone, never intentionally hurts anyone, loves God and goes to church, and so on.

The problem and question you must answer without hesitation:

Have you really given your life to Jesus Christ?

I prayed almost nonstop for the next two days about everything possible and asked God so many questions about so many things.

He must have thought I had lost my mind. Finally, I knew it had happened. God had heard me and Christ was there to allow me to be born again. It was the middle of the morning, January 28, the day of my second wedding anniversary. What a remarkable, wonderful, uplifting feeling. I had truly given my life to Christ for the first time in my life and more importantly, understood what it meant. I can never forget that moment.

Life without alcohol. I had been drinking for over 40 years, virtually nonstop. My life revolved around alcohol. I thought about it all the time. I use to love those little tests you read about that determined if you were an alcoholic. What a joke. If they only knew half the life I lived drinking, they would have to come up with a whole new name for the disease. I would imagine very few people drank as much as I did. The scary thing is nobody really had a clue about the extent of my abuse.

I'm not going to reminisce with you too much about all my years of drinking. When I do look back, **it is hard not to associate alcohol with every bad thing that ever happened to me or my family.** That is pretty sad to ponder.

I will be the first to tell you that I had one heck of a time throughout my life with alcohol and was definitely the life of the party. Most of the time it was impossible for people to really have a clue about how much I had been drinking. I was a professional, functioning drinker.

I was lucky enough, through those years, to never get in any serious trouble over booze. Never had all the DUIs, car wrecks, fights, and so on, that a lot of my friends ended up with. God was definitely watching over me.

It is almost shameful to even make a stab at how much money I spent on booze. I could have probably retired at 30 instead of 39.

How do you stop drinking after 40 years of addiction? Once again, I did not specifically pray to God for this. I knew it was up to me. He was giving me, and I mean me, not him, an opportunity to change my life for the better and to live. He had just saved my life, but it was up to me to walk away from the cliff. It was right there, ready and begging for me to jump. **It was my faith in God and my family that allowed me to conquer the demon. Satan had just lost one of his best buddies.**

I will describe, in some detail, the struggle to adjust to not drinking, because I do think this could help anyone who struggles with life-changing challenges.

First, I stopped pretty much cold turkey and did not get involved with any support group. I wanted to do this on my own. Not saying that is the right way to do it, or suggesting it. I wanted all the responsibility to fall directly on me. **No one to blame but myself.**

My biggest challenge was to somehow not let this change my personality. I liked the way I was and I had been very successful with the way I handled myself personally and professionally. Would I turn into a wall flower without my buddy, booze? Did I have to have a drink to be personable? Even worse, did I have to have a drink to play music and sing in front of an audience?

This was some pretty terrifying stuff to be hit with.

I'm going to say it took me almost two years to really get comfortable with my new self. Most people say they never really saw any change other than a much improved person. Bottom line: there was life without alcohol. I never thought it could or would happen. I just imagined that eventually something bad would happen and it would all be over. Doesn't that scare the hell out of you!

I hope people reading this and relating to my story find the strength to deal with their demons and open up a whole new better life. It can and did happen for me.

You know all that corny stuff about my family and how we were always so close and all that mushy stuff I wrote about in the beginning of the book?

The family

Well, they are the reason I was not going to fail. I refused to let them down. It was not about how I felt or survived. It was about not making them suffer, if something happened to me. That was all the motivation I needed.

It took two years for my feet to get back to almost normal. You're thinking what in the heck is he talking about now? Because of all the drinking, I had come down with gout in both my feet, more times than I can remember. If you know anything about gout, once is enough for anyone's lifetime. It is a crippling, mind-numbing inflammation in the joints of your body. I've had friends say they would rather die than have gout again. It is caused by numerous things, but excessive drinking is a major one.

The other problem with gout is that when it goes away, it leaves crystal deposits in the affected area that never go away. They just build up in your body with each episode. My feet were almost deformed. I could barely wear shoes by the time my liver failed.

I had to take medicine for two years to dissolve all the sediment in my feet.

That really is about all I want to say about drinking and that's a good "footnote" to wind it down on. No pun intended.

Seriously, I could write a whole book about this subject, alone, and still never really cover it all.

Final word: **Avoid alcohol if you can, and in moderation if you must.**

To end with a very happy and wonderful conclusion to this chapter, I have to brag about my final marriage, which occurred on January 28, 2010, to Diane Payne.

I had just broken off an 11-year relationship with a wonderful woman whom I loved dearly. Obviously, I was not willing or able to commit to another engagement for reasons I don't think I really know or ever will know. Maybe it was the previous engagement fiasco or a midlife crisis, again. For whatever reason, it just was not meant to be and I somehow knew it.

My 30-year high-school reunion was coming up in the summer of 2007. I was always one of the volunteers who helped orchestrate and organize our reunions. We would get a group of around 10 to 15 people to help put everything together. A few months before each reunion, we would start meeting once a week at various bars in the neighborhood, in the evening, to discuss our progress. We always had a blast putting these things together.

This is where I reintroduced myself to my bride to be. Diane and I would hang around after the meetings to have a few more cocktails and talk about old times.

The funny thing is that she was our homecoming queen in high school and I was always considered the anti-Christ. What a pair. Sounds like my folks. Things gradually progressed and we ended up going to the reunion together. Needless to say, we were the talk of the party. All night long I kept hearing, "You're dating Tommy Lawhead?" as if she were with some wild animal or criminal. Nobody could believe it.

We dated for about three years and got married in January 2010. This time there was no doubt about engagement, marriage or commitment. I couldn't let her get away. Oh, and what a great family she has and now I have. Diane has truly been a blessing and continues to make me feel like a king in our home.

Wedding, Tom and Diane

Who said God doesn't challenge us?

At the end of these three years I ended up:

1. Never being able to do again what I had enjoyed more than almost anything in my life: drinking.

2. For almost six months having no sex drive due to all my medications, something I had enjoyed more than number one.

3. Robbed of over half my life's savings.

Who said God isn't there for us?

After I gave my life to Christ:

1. I've never been happier and healthier in my life since I stopped drinking.

2. Diane and I are back stronger than ever, romantically.

3. I was able to invest my pension money from the bank and regain almost all that had been stolen from me.

Role reversal is something I never thought about or even considered dealing with during my life. What do I mean by this? I'm talking about aging parents. I decided **you haven't lived until you have had to change your parent's diapers.** I know that sounds sick, but I've been there. It is much more humiliating to the parent than the child, trust me again on this one.

Fortunately, for the most part, my parents stayed pretty healthy. But there were occasions when all four boys had to come up to the plate and pay all those years back to our parents. And all four did. We almost fought over who was going to come to their aid. **I'm talking about wanting to help, not dodging it.** We all knew how much they had done for us, so it was never considered an inconvenience to help out, although it did get tough at times. We were fortunate that Allen and Mike were medical doctors. That was really a godsend.

I don't know how other families deal with the hospital system and doctors without having somebody close who is in the business. The communication barriers and lack of understanding of the health-care system are overwhelming.

Just become very aware—if you haven't already—**of the heavy responsibility caring for your parents can become.** You will be challenged financially, physically and emotionally. Hopefully, spiritually, you will be aided.

The year 2012 ended tragically for me with the **death of my mother.** She came down with pneumonia in October and had to go to the hospital. She died 30 days later. She was 86 years old. What a loss to this world and our family.

Tom's mother, "Tutie"

She was a magnificent woman and as strong as you will ever see. When she died, she had already lost both of her legs to diabetes, which never slowed her down. She had more energy and vitality than anyone I've ever known.

She was the backbone of the entire family. What a matriarch! Everybody loved her and she loved everybody. Her sons were her whole life. Everything we did, good or bad, we worried about how Tutie would respond. That was her nickname and that's what everybody called her. We hadn't called her mom in over 30 years.

It was all about pleasing her, as far as we were concerned. She was also as tough as they come. You did not want to get on her bad side. She took no prisoners.

I was fortunate enough to be holding her hand when she passed away. That is an experience you can never share with someone who has not been there. One minute there is this loving, beautiful woman you have spent your whole life worshiping and in a second, there is this lifeless body, just lying there. You can literally see her soul taking off and leaving behind a sort of carrying case. I know that sounds awful, but those were my feelings and thoughts at the time. It was a wonderful experience. We knew she had given her life to Christ and she was on her way to be with him. You couldn't help but be in awe of the whole moment. I was happy for her.

Takeaways to Live By

47. Give your life to Jesus Christ.

48. Times will try your soul and you need to be ready.

49. Never underestimate the power of prayer.

50. Regardless of your challenges in life, try not to become discouraged.

51. Family is the greatest thing to have around in times of need. Don't ever forget that.

52. Think about some of the worst things that have ever happened to you, and whether alcohol was involved.

What You Can Do Next

Read the book again. This time, take a few notes. Takeaways are meant to be picked through and pondered. Hopefully, you stumbled across a few that stuck. My greatest hope and desire is that you read something that you maybe haven't thought about before. Maybe you read something that gives you a whole new perspective on life or a relationship.

Let me leave you with some general thoughts and observations about where I've been, where I am and where I plan on going.

Where I've been. Pretty much everywhere I've wanted to go and more. My book gives you a candid snapshot of my life so far.

Where I am now. I mentioned in my introduction that I now play and sing in various health-care facilities—I mean everything from people with Alzheimer's, dementia and autism to just plain elderly, as well as abandoned, mentally, physically and emotionally ill and indigent and special needs individuals of all sorts. I'm seeing just about everything imaginable.

What I didn't describe in my introduction is the enormous effect this is having on me.

The days I spend here playing and singing for hours drain me physically. It drains me spiritually, emotionally and psychologically just observing everything going on around me.

When I get home, my mind is spinning, trying to make some sense of it all. I think about all the staff, nurses, ministers and doctors in these hospitals and homes and what effect it has on their lives and their families. I think about the bus drivers who carry these individuals back and forth. I think about the janitors in these facilities and all the volunteers, like me, who give freely of their time and money. What drives them to be here and what makes them come back?

Since playing in these facilities, lots of my friends have asked my advice about adult care. There is just no easy answer and since I'm so involved on both sides, I hesitate to comment. I'll just say: Do everything you can for your loved ones and keep them as close to home for as long as you can. There often does come a time when outside help is the only answer. There are many great places out there. Just do your homework.

These are not the most pleasant of circumstances for anyone. I share this for those of you who have not yet been exposed to this side of life but will be in some way at some point in your life. I also share it, especially, for those who are right in the midst of it.

After being exposed day in and day out to the overwhelming circumstances in these different facilities and seeing the pain and suffering daily, *blessed* is the only word that comes to mind when determining "where I am."

What you can do next, after reading the book again: **Volunteer! I challenge** you to consider spending some time volunteering in some of these places I have described: hospitals, nursing homes, adult day care, special needs facilities, and so on.

It will change your life.

This experience is leading me spiritually where I've never been before or imagined. Kind of like *Star Trek*. To boldly go … You get it.

Five years ago I would have laughed if someone had told me I would be performing in "old folks' homes."

More important, I am seeing first hand, every day, people who are approaching death. I find myself talking to anyone and everyone I can, trying to get some sense of their relationship with God. This is not an easy thing for me, but I feel driven. What a great opportunity to share the word of God!

The good news, at least in my experiences, is that many are saved and even more want to be.

God bless!

I also try to get a good sense of the family relationships with these individuals. Is there a closeness with the family or are there issues that should be and haven't been resolved, especially if they are nearing their death?

It tears me apart to hear some of these folks talk about their relationships with certain family members, how they never speak to a particular family member. Some refuse to communicate with a sibling, child or parent because of some issue or argument that happened years ago. The sad part is when they actually share with me the issue or circumstance causing the problem, it is miniscule in comparison to what they are sacrificing and missing out on. That is a travesty.

Now, I do know there are situations where there are extremely serious issues that need to be resolved. This takes much more effort but needs to be done. You take the first, second and third steps. You step as far as it takes.

Literally unimaginable to me is what goes on in someone's mind after they have lost a loved one they have basically disowned or abandoned for whatever reason. Please take ownership in reconciling a situation like this. It may take months or years, but do not give up. You will be thankful in the end. Look at it this way: everyone loses if no one addresses the situation. Make everyone a winner. You be the hero in the background. Make it your mission to reconcile the family. **Be the "silent hero."**

Where I plan on going. Fishing! Hope you enjoyed our journey together.

Final Takeaway

53. Make a difference.

Take all this away and start loving life!

The Lawhead brothers: Doug, Tom, Al and Mike

Tom's backyard view at Spences Point, Lake Murray